Making your Children's Clothes PENNY PINCHERS

Contents

Introduction

In the past, children's clothes were difficult to make as they were really replicas of grown-up clothes in miniature and very intricate in design. They were more often than not uncomfortable to wear as well, as the fabrics were too heavy and coarse, irritating a child's delicate skin.

Today, the picture is totally different. The clothes are very simple in style and easy to make. The major pattern companies, McCall's, Vogue, Butterick, Style and Simplicity, have an excellent variety of children's designs to choose from, covering all aspects of clothing which are suitable for children of all ages from newborn babies and toddlers to older children. Until recently fabrics were a problem, but now fabric manufacturers have realised that the type of materials, colours and designs offered to grown-ups were unsuitable for children. There is a wide variety of exciting and pretty fabrics just right for children's wear available in the shops.

This book is designed to give helpful hints and information on sewing children's clothes and saving the pennies. Careful planning when creating a child's wardrobe, by choice of fabrics and colour co-ordination, is the secret of success, enabling you to clothe your child as you would wish while keeping within your budget. By making them yourself, you will also be able to afford many more clothes for your child which will give the garments a longer lease of life as they will suffer less wear and tear. With the advent of marvellous electric sewing machines, children's clothes can be made up very quickly indeed as the machines do most of the work for you. However, not all of us are lucky enough to possess one, so techniques of sewing by hand are included here as well. The end results will be just the same but will take a little more time and patience. I hope the book will encourage sewing beginners as well. Once you understand the basic sewing techniques and terminology you will see how simple it is and sewing will become a pleasure rather than a chore—and you will save money at the same time.

Choose the correct size of pattern by consulting the Standard Measurement Chart at the back of the pattern catalogues and always have a fitting before finally machining up the outfit. Check that your fabric is suitable for the design by consulting the fabric recommendations on the back of the pattern envelope. Extra fabric will be required for matching checks, stripes and one-way designs depending on the size of the repeat.

Before starting to machine, always check the tension and stitch length on a test sample of the fabric and ensure that you have the correct needle : for stretchable knitted fabrics use a ball-point needle ; for delicate fabrics, eg lawn, batiste, lightweight cottons, use a fine sharp needle ; for heavier fabrics you will need a stronger needle.

Select your thread : use a synthetic thread for synthetic fibres ; cotton for pure cotton and lightweight wools and mercerised cotton for heavier weight, natural fabrics ; or use a multi-purpose thread such as Drima or Dewhurst Star. Use a special thick top-stitching thread for top-stitching or the effect of the stitching will be lost. Always choose the thread carefully, choosing a slightly darker shade than the fabric as the thread will come up lighter as it comes off the full reel.

Machine seams from the top towards the hem. On curved seams, such as armholes and cuffs, machine from the inside. When joining a gathered skirt or frill to the main part of the outfit, machine with the gathers uppermost to keep them smooth. Always machine fabrics with a pile, such as velvet and corduroy, 'with' the pile to avoid the foot marking the fabric.

In order to protect the pile when working with slippery fabrics or with velvet, it is a good idea to place tissue paper between the two layers before machining the seam. When using fabrics which can stretch out of shape, tack tissue paper underneath. The tissue can easily be torn away after machining.

There are some marvellous quick and easy sewing aids on the market such as hemming web, so you can just iron your hem into place, buttonsnaps which avoid the labour of making buttonholes, and self-adhesive fastenings. Decorative elastic is available in various widths perfect for waistbands, cuffs and around the bottom of jackets.

Fitting

The fit of a garment has great bearing on the finished appearance of an outfit. It is the difference between clothes looking home-made and the professional touch. Careful measurement beforehand can save a lot of heartache. Children are impatient and not prepared to stand still for lots of adjustments to be made. Accurate notes at the beginning should ensure that only one fitting is needed, when the garment is tacked up, before the final machining or sewing.

Children's wear does not need the tailored fit of grown-up attire. Clothes tend to hang loosely from the shoulders, controlled either with a tie belt or an elastic casing to give them any slight shaping required. Therefore the shoulder, chest and neckline fit, together with the finished length, are the most important factors. Patterns should be selected by the breast/chest measurement as other areas are easy to adjust once this fit has been accomplished.

Children's patterns come in various figure types: toddlers, children, girls and boys. It must be remembered that the sizes refer to the child's measurements and not to his age. To ascertain one's choice of size and type of pattern, take the following measurements and compare them with the Standard Measurement Chart found at the back of pattern catalogues. Firstly it is important to locate the waist. This can be difficult as children are fairly straight up and down. But it will be needed not only as a measurement in itself but also to calculate the finished length of clothes. Mark the waistline by tying a piece of string or narrow ribbon around it and take the following measurements:

Overall height standing against a wall without shoes
Breast/chest placing the tape measure under the arms straight across the back and front
Waist over the top of the tie
Back waist length from the 'bump' at the base of the neck—ie the vertebra at the top of the spine— to the waist tie

To measure the finished lengths of the clothes, take the back length of dresses from the base of the neck; skirts, pants, and shorts from the waistline tie over the hip; and sleeve length from the tip of the shoulder to the wrist.

Toddlers' and children's breast and waist measurements are usually the same although the clothes vary in length. Toddlers' patterns begin at a smaller size and are graded for a figure between a baby and a child, so clothes are shorter and pants have extra ease to go over nappies. Girls' patterns are designed for a girl who has not begun to mature but has acquired a waistline. Boys up to a 65cm (25½in) chest come into the children's category. For boys' sizes 7–12 (see the measurement chart at the back of the catalogues), who have not reached the age of adolescence, you will also need the following measurements:

Around the bottom of the neck
Around the largest part of the hip between the waist and crotch
Shoulder length from the bottom of the neck to the top of the shoulder
Outside leg from the waist to finished

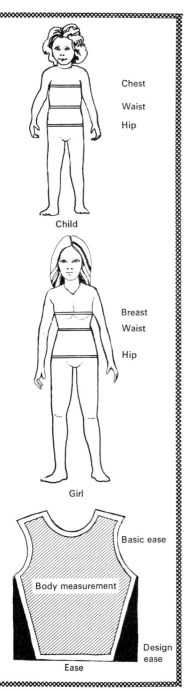

Child

Girl

Ease
Body measurement
Basic ease
Design ease

length
Inside leg from crotch to finished length
Crotch depth, which is the difference between the inside and outside leg measurements.

Ease

Having bought your pattern, compare the child's measurements with the tissue by measuring from seamline to seamline, so if any adjustments are necessary these can be made to the tissue before cutting out your fabric. It is most important to remember that all patterns have a certain amount of ease built into the design to allow for natural movement and the tissue should be slightly larger than actual measurements to account for this.

The amount of ease will vary according to the type of fabric recommended for the design listed on the pattern envelope (knitted fabrics have less ease because of their natural elasticity than woven fabrics) and the type of design.

Room should also be allowed if sweaters, etc are to be worn under the outfit and body measurements should be taken over the top of these garments. Ease will also be greater in all-in-one outfits, such as jumpsuits and dungarees, to avoid your child being rubbed or cut painfully when moving. Careful note should be taken of the front and back crotch lengths.

Patterns designed for stretch fabrics normally carry a guide to show how much elasticity there should be in the material. As the amount of stretch does vary in different fabrics, it is essential that the correct one is chosen, or the design will become distorted.

Basic Wardrobe

Layette for a Newborn Baby

Baby clothes should be light, warm and loose fitting so that the child's limbs are not constricted. Babies have very delicate skins so fabrics must be fine and soft to avoid irritation. As their clothes will be washed frequently, choose easy-care materials such as lightweight cotton, batiste, voile, challis, lightweight wools, cotton flannel, cotton knits and soft towelling. If possible, ensure that the clothes are washed in pure soap rather than in strong detergents which again may irritate delicate skin. Do not choose harsh colours which will detract from the baby's tiny features and pale complexion. White and cream are an obvious choice, but if you would like to use other colours, pick mute shades of blue, lemon and pink, avoiding harsh colours at all costs. Elaborate trimmings are not advisable as they have the same unkind effect as strong colours. Keep clothes very simple, highlighting edges with blanket stitch, fine narrow lace, or scallops, which will give a pretty finishing touch. Only use simple embroidery stitches such as satin, chain, and lazy daisy, which don't look fussy on small clothes.

You will find excellent layettes for your baby in the major pattern companies' catalogues which you can make up while waiting for the birth. In general, it is worth remembering that raglan sleeves and sleeves cut in one with the garment are a good idea as they give extra room around the upper arm. Choose clothes which hang loosely, either gathered into the neck or into a high yoke to give lots of room for movement.

Basically, you will need a long dress and coat which can also be used for the baby's christening ; a bonnet or hat to keep the head warm ; an all in one cover-up, clothing hands and feet, with a hood for the head ; a nightgown, a dressing gown, a bib, a matinée jacket, a short day dress for a girl, and a small jacket and pants to go over a nappy for a boy ; bootees, mittens, a vest and a shawl. I have not mentioned nappies as they can be made from 1 sq m (1 sq yd) of towelling, but it is probably quicker and easier to buy them.

Basic Wardrobe for Young Children

For children whose clothes are going to have to suffer more wear and tear than babies' clothes, it is a good idea from a budget point of view to include quite a few separates. These can be worn with different shirts and sweaters so you can swing the changes to get several different looks from a few basic clothes. Keep one outfit for 'best', a dress for a girl and a suit for a boy, which is not going to end up covered in mud, or with the pockets torn off during robust play, just when you are in a hurry to go somewhere special. Also give them a change from school uniform when they come home so that they can relax and let off their high spirits without fear of getting dirty.

When deciding on a basic wardrobe choose colours carefully so that they can be co-ordinated and a new jumper will not necessarily need to have a new skirt or trousers to go with it.

For a girl, you will need pinafore dresses, skirts, blouses and sweaters,

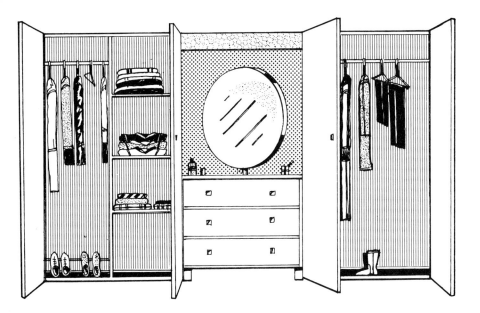

day dresses and perhaps a long party dress, a nightie and a dressing-gown. For a boy you will need one good suit, a tie, trousers, shorts, a casual jacket, shirts and sweaters, pyjamas and a dressing gown. Dungarees, jumpsuits, jeans and T-shirts can be worn by either sex. A coat will be needed, and an anorak or poncho, a mackintosh, socks, shoes and wellingtons.

School uniforms are expensive to buy and it is well worth while checking with your child's school to see if they have chosen a pattern and fabric for their uniform which you can then make up far more cheaply yourself.

Hardwearing and easy-care fabrics are a must for children's clothes as they spend so much time in the washing machine. Now there is a wide choice of fabrics on the market at economic prices suitable for children's wear, ranging from lightweight cottons, lawn, batiste, gingham, synthetic blends and mixtures to duck, drill, gaberdine, denim, corduroy, wools, wool blends, and their synthetic counterparts which all come in a variety of colours and designs.

For a tall, thin child, choose clothes which give an illusion of extra width such as smock dresses, empire-line or waisted dresses with gathered skirts, skirts with frills, short puff sleeves or long full sleeves gathered at the sleevehead. Bold prints and checks and horizontal stripes are very suitable.

For a plump child, choose a straighter silhouette such as A-line dresses flaring from a high yoke or from the shoulders and set in sleeves. Small prints and checks and lengthwise stripes are the most suitable.

Waterproof fabric for raincoats and ponchos is not widely available in this country. However, most good dry cleaners will proof the clothes for you after you have made them up.

Pattern Markings and Terminology

The major pattern companies all have clear markings on the design tissue to ensure the garment goes together correctly and easily. A clear understanding of this terminology will aid quick and easy making up of a garment.

The Selvage Edge

This is the narrow woven strip on either side of the width of the fabric.

Fabric Grain

It is most important that your fabric grain is perfect to ensure that the garment hangs properly when completed. If the material is off-grain and not straightened out before cutting the pattern pieces, the fabric will pucker and bulge and never hang correctly. The grain is the direction in which the threads of the fabric run. In woven fabrics, the lengthwise grain comprises the threads running parallel to the selvage and the crosswide grain comprises the threads running across the fabric, under and over the lengthwise threads at right angles. In knit fabrics, the vertical rows of loops are the lengthwise grain and the crosswise grain runs perpendicular to this, as in woven fabrics. To cut on the bias, first find the true bias of the fabric by folding the material diagonally so that the crosswise threads are parallel to the selvage. The grainline will be shown on the tissue by a thick arrow with points at both ends. Whether the tissue is to be placed on the lengthwise or crosswise grain or bias of the fabric will also be indicated.

If your fabric is off-grain, there are two ways to correct this. With the help of a friend, hold one end of the fabric and pull the material on the true bias in the opposite direction to the higher off-grain edges. Keep stretching in this way along the selvage edges until the crosswise threads are at ninety degrees or perpendicular to the lengthwise threads. If the fabric is too thick and strong to straighten in this way, as wools would be, it has to be pulled and blocked into shape while pressing the material using a damp pressing cloth or steam iron.

Fabric Layouts

When laying out your pattern pieces, study the instruction sheet carefully to see whether the fabric is laid out flat in a single layer, whether the two selvage edges should be together giving a lengthwise fold, or whether the fabric is folded on the crosswise grain giving a crosswise fold.

Notches

Notches are triangular markings which are vital to ensure that the correct pieces go together and to avoid mistakes, such as a sleeve being put in the wrong way round. You may also be required to gather between two

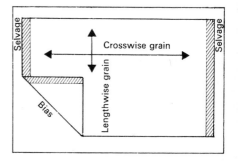

notches or ease in the fabric. Transfer these markings either by cutting out the notches outside the seam allowance—two or three notches can be cut together as one shape—or by making small snips in the seam allowance.

Small and Large Dots

These are also very important guidelines during construction. They mark points in a seam to show how far it should be sewn up, such as to the bottom of the zip opening, or to where a pocket is to be inserted into the seam allowance. They are used as markers for gathering and often matched up with seams, especially when setting in a sleeve to match the sleevehead with the shoulder seam. They mark darts and the positioning of pattern pieces such as patch pockets. These markings should be transferred to the fabric by making two tacks to form a cross. Use double strands of thread and leave fairly long tails of thread at either end of the stitch. You can also use proper tailor's tacks. Work these stitches with tacking thread of a different colour from the fabric so that they will show up clearly.

Seam Allowances and Cutting Lines

The seam allowance is clearly shown on designs from all the major pattern companies. This is normally 1.5cm ($\frac{5}{8}$in) and shown as a broken line inside the thick cutting-line. When checking your measurements against the tissue to see if any adjustment is necessary, remember to measure from seamline to seamline and not between the cutting-lines. Most modern sewing machines will have a space gauge beside the foot which helps you keep an even seam. If there is no seam allowance inside, only a single line, check to see whether this line should be placed on a fold and do not cut it. Transfer the seam allowance to your fabric, making a series of tacks using double strands of thread and leaving fairly long tails, or make tailor's tacks.

Darts

A dart will be shown by dots at intervals along two broken converging lines ending in a point with a single dot. Darts control fullness and give shape to garments to make them fit. These markings should be transferred to the fabric using tacks with long tails of thread at either end of the first and last stitch for the broken lines. Double tacks forming a cross should mark the dots or use tailor's tacks with different coloured thread.

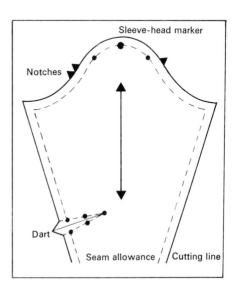

Sleeve-head marker

Notches

Dart

Seam allowance / / Cutting line

Pattern Markings and Terminology

Right and wrong side

The right and wrong sides of the fabric are usually differentiated by shading. This is most important if the material is printed only on one side. A pattern piece, to be placed face down on the fabric, will also be marked by shading so check carefully with the sewing directions on the instruction sheet to find out what sort of markings they have used.

Grading

When you have two or more layers of fabric, and possibly interfacing too, the seam has to be graded to reduce the bulk and prevent an unsightly ridge forming and showing through to the right side of the garment when the seam is pressed. The layers of fabric have to be cut away in differing widths with the widest layer next to the outside fabric and the interfacing trimmed as close as possible to the seamline.

Interfacing

Interfacing is used to give a crisp finish to garments and keep them in shape. It is used in collars, cuffs, openings which have to bear the strain of fastenings and waistbands. Interfacings vary in weight and construction and it is important that you choose the sort compatible with your fabric. Woven interfacings should be used for woven fabrics. Use transparent interfacings for sheer fabrics. There are also lightweight, medium and heavy qualities and a special thick interfacing for waistbands. For stretchable knitted fabrics use a non-woven interfacing with a flexibility to complement the fabric and prevent puckering while still providing the necessary stability. Both woven and non-woven interfacings come in iron-on versions, which is a great time-saver, but do be careful that your fabric is suitable and will not shrivel away when a hot iron is applied. Interfacing is also used on hems of very stretchy knits to prevent the fabric from puckering. When applying by hand, tack into place on the wrong side of the fabric 1.3cm ($\frac{1}{2}$in) in from the raw edges and hem stitch along a foldline.

Transferring Markings on to the Fabric

It is extremely important that all markings on the tissue—darts, notches, dots, seam allowances, pleats and tucks—are transferred on to the fabric before the tissue is removed. There are several ways to do this including tacking, as already described. Two other quick and easy ways are to use either pins and tailor's chalk or dressmaker's carbon and a tracing wheel.

The former method can be used on most fabrics as the chalk marks come off easily when the outfit is washed or dry cleaned. With the tissue facing upwards, insert pins through the markings and continue straight down through the layers of fabric. Carefully turn the tissue and fabric over so that all the pins are pointing straight up in the air. On a hard, flat working surface draw lines connecting the pins with a ruler and tailor's chalk. Turn the piece

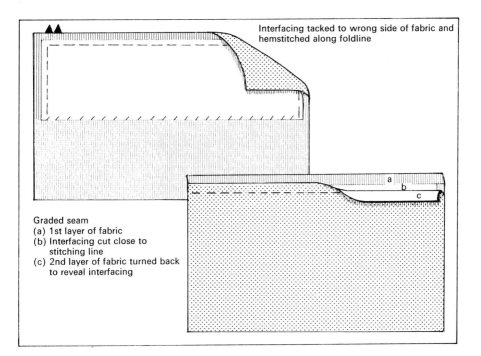

Interfacing tacked to wrong side of fabric and hemstitched along foldline

Graded seam
(a) 1st layer of fabric
(b) Interfacing cut close to stitching line
(c) 2nd layer of fabric turned back to reveal interfacing

over with the tissue facing upwards and gently remove the pattern piece pulling the pins through the tissue so that they remain in the fabric. Draw in the lines connecting the pin heads.

When using dressmaker's carbon and a tracing wheel, the markings have to be transferred to the wrong side of the fabric. This method cannot be used on transparent or very pale fine fabrics as the carbon lines would show through to the right side. They do not wash out. Select light-coloured carbon paper for dark fabrics and vice versa for light-coloured fabrics. To mark two layers of fabric at the same time, cut a strip of carbon 7.5cm (3in) wide by 25.5cm (10in) long and fold it in half with the carbon side exposed. Put the bottom half under the top layer of fabric and the other between the top layer of fabric and the tissue. Draw along the markings with the tracing wheel using a ruler where necessary.

With and Without Nap

A fabric with nap has a one-way design, pile, nap or shading such as corduroy, velvet and fur, and all the pattern pieces must go in the same direction. Test which way the pile runs by gently rubbing your hand over the surface of the fabric. Velvet should be cut with the pile running towards the top of the outfit and corduroy and fur with the pile going towards the hem. A fabric without nap is one with a design going either way and without pile, nap or shading so pattern pieces can go in opposite directions, which often saves on the amount of fabric required.

Hems

The hem, normally the final part of construction, should not be finished in a rush at the last minute. In a way it is almost the most important aspect, making the difference between a perfectly finished garment and one which looks home-made. It is difficult to persuade a child to stand straight and still, and it is worth a bribe so you can mark the hem accurately using a ruler and tailor's chalk or pins, the secret of a successful, even hem rather than one which dips and sways.

Always allow the garment to hang for at least twenty-four hours before turning up the hem in case the fabric should drop, making the hem uneven. Make sure the child is standing on a hard, flat surface and wearing any bulky clothes which will usually be worn underneath. Turn up the hem on the marking-line and pin into place with pins perpendicular to the folded edge, removing any marking pins as you go.

Tack evenly, close to the folded edge. Take out the pins and press the hem on the inside on the folded edge. Cut the hem to an even width.

With very stretchy fabrics and loosely-woven knits it can be a good idea to interface the hem to give it extra stability. Cut the interfacing on the bias 5mm ($\frac{1}{4}$in) wider than the finished hem and mark a line 2cm ($\frac{3}{4}$in) in from one of the long edges. Place this line to the foldline of the hem on the wrong side of the fabric and sew into place 5mm ($\frac{1}{4}$in) below the foldline, catching the top edge of the interfacing to the garment seams. Turn up the hem

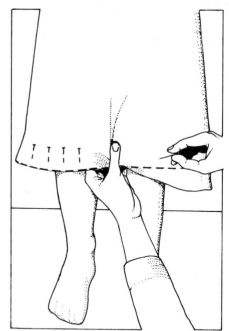

Turn up hem on marking line

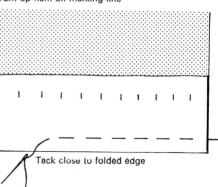

Tack close to folded edge

Trim hem

on the foldline and sew into place.

If the upper edge of the hem is wider than the garment, which can easily happen in children's clothes when a large hem is being allowed to account for growth, the extra fullness can be shrunk out. Run a gathering thread round the hem just below the top edge. Turn up the hem and pin to the seams, pulling up the thread in between to fit and adjusting the fullness evenly. Put thick paper between the hem and the garment fabric and press with a steam iron on the inside. The paper will prevent a mark appearing on the right side of the garment.

As children seem to shoot up at a rate of knots, always allow as deep a hem as possible and slip stitch by hand so that it can be let down easily. Do not machine the hem as this may leave a mark on the fabric when you try to let it down. If the style of the outfit allows it, make a double hem. Make the first hem as described, then turn up the amount of the hem again and slip stitch into place.

Hems

There are several kinds of hems and which one you choose really depends on the type of garment and weight of fabric, as the object is to make the hem as invisible as possible.

A regular or dressmaker's hem is suitable for most fabrics and styles. First neaten the raw edge by the method most suited to your material (see the section on seam finishes). Tack the hem in place, 1.3cm ($\frac{1}{2}$in) below the upper edge. Turn the fabric back on this stitching-line and sew, picking up a thread of the garment and making a small diagonal stitch into the hem. Do not pull the stitches too tight as this will make the hem pucker. When the hem is completed, take out the tacking threads and press it from the inside.

If the fabric is likely to fray, the edge of the hem can be encased in bias seam binding. With right sides together, stitch the binding to the top of the hem and if necessary, trim the seam to 3mm ($\frac{1}{8}$in). Fold the tape over the top of the raw edge of the hem and press.

Join the binding to the hem, stitching along the seamline on the right side. Fold the hem back to just below the stitching-line and sew into place with invisible stitches as before.

Very fine, delicate fabrics, such as baby clothes, should be finished with a tiny rolled hem. Using a machine or continuous running stitch, sew round the garment 3mm ($\frac{1}{8}$in) from the bottom edge, trimming the fabric close to the stitching-line. Roll the edge of the fabric between your thumb and first finger to cover the raw edge and secure with tiny hemming stitches. Alternatively, a very narrow hem can be made which is useful for shirts and blouses as well as in places where a normal hem would be too bulky. First turn under 3mm ($\frac{1}{8}$in) on the raw edge and stitch close to the edge. Fold under the same amount again and sew into place with tiny hemming stitches.

A useful hem for children's clothes which are going to spend most of their time in the washing machine is a turned and stitched hem, but this can only be applied to fabrics which do not show through to the right side. Make an even row of tacking stitches 6mm

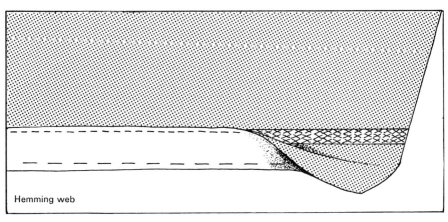

Hemming web

($\frac{1}{4}$in) below the top edge of the hem and turn under the raw edge on the stitching-line. Machine close to the folded edge, press and remove the tacking threads. Turn up the hem and tack into position. Sew the hem into place with invisible stitches.

A smooth and simple finish can be used on shorts and blouses made in fabrics which do not fray. Either machine around the bottom 1.3cm ($\frac{1}{2}$in) from the raw edge and trim the fabric with pinking shears 6mm ($\frac{1}{4}$in) below the stitching-line and leave flat or turn up the trimmed edge on the stitching-line and sew into place close to the folded edge.

Felt, of course, is a marvellous time-saving fabric for skirts and capes if your child is not going to outgrow the garment before it wears out. As the fabric does not fray, there is no need to neaten the seams or turn up the hem. Simply cut the skirt to the desired finished length taking care to keep it even.

There are two quick and easy ways of turning up a hem if it is likely that the clothes will be worn out before they become too short. Using either of these methods it is almost impossible to let down a hem at a later date. Either a strip of hemming web can be placed between the hem and the garment, which will stick the two together when they are ironed, or a hem can be turned up and top stitched into place giving a decorative finish to the garment. Neaten the raw edge and turn under 1.5cm ($\frac{5}{8}$in) hem. Tack and machine two rows of top stitching, the first 6mm ($\frac{1}{4}$in) from the folded edge and the second 6mm ($\frac{1}{4}$in) above this. Remove the tacking stitches and press.

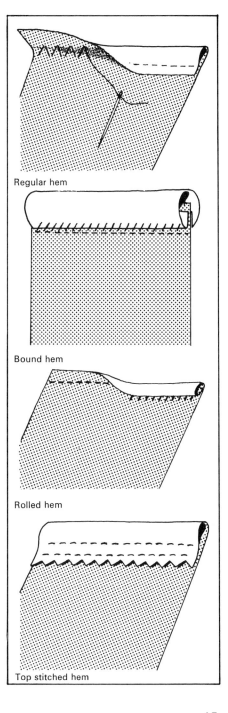

Regular hem

Bound hem

Rolled hem

Top stitched hem

15

Trousers

Trousers, like skirts, are very useful separates for a child's wardrobe as they can be worn with different shirts, blouses, T-shirts and sweaters, giving various looks from one basic garment.

The fit of trousers so that they hang correctly and are neither too loose nor too baggy is most important. The measurements you will need are waist, hip, thigh, inside and outside leg and the crotch length. The waist should fit comfortably and remember to allow enough ease on the hips and thighs so that the child can bend and sit down. The crotch length is most important and should be taken sitting down. Measure from the waist to the middle of the crotch both from the front and from the back, taking the tape-measure through the child's legs. Although the crotch length on the pattern may be the same as the overall crotch measurement, children tend to have round tummies and the front crotch length should be lengthened to account for this. On the other hand, if the child has a large behind the back crotch will have to be extended. Obviously, the crotch does not want to be hanging down around the knees but *do* allow enough ease for natural movement and for your child to sit down without being cut in two.

Probably the most sensible waists for children's trousers are made either with an elastic casing or with a waistband made of decorative elastic, which will stretch as the child begins to grow. With an elastic casing, the elastic can always be removed when the waist becomes too tight, and a longer length can be inserted.

To make the casing, allow a 2cm ($\frac{3}{4}$in) turning at the top edge of the trousers. Turn under 3mm ($\frac{1}{8}$in) to the wrong side on the top edge and press. Turn under a further 1.5cm ($\frac{5}{8}$in) and press. Stitch close to the folded edge at the top and then stitch again close to the bottom edge leaving a 2.5cm (1in) gap to insert the elastic through. Cut a length of 1.3cm ($\frac{1}{2}$in) wide elastic so that it fits comfortably around the waist plus an extra 1.3cm ($\frac{1}{2}$in). Attach a safety pin to one end of the elastic and thread it through the casing. Overlap the ends of the elastic by 6mm ($\frac{1}{4}$in) on each end and sew together securely. Hem the remainder of the casing to close the gap.

When using decorative elastic to control fullness at the waist, cut a length to fit comfortably around the waist plus an extra 2cm ($\frac{3}{4}$in). Turn in the ends by 3mm ($\frac{1}{8}$in) to neaten. If the opening is at the centre front, have the left side of the elastic level with the left side of the opening and the right side extending by 1.3cm ($\frac{1}{2}$in) for a girl and vice versa for a boy. Attach to the right side of the trousers with the bottom of the elastic just covering the seam allowance. Machine on the seamline and sew hooks and eyes or snaps on the underside of the overlap to close the waistband.

To elasticate trouser waistband: turn down top of trousers to inside and stitch to form casing, leaving a gap in the centre back to insert elastic

Trousers

If a self-fabric waistband is preferred to give the trousers a more tailored look, cut a rectangle of fabric on the lengthwise grain so that it fits comfortably around the waist plus an extra 4.5cm (1¾in). It should be twice the finished width of the desired waistband with an added 3.2cm (1¼in). Cut out a piece of interfacing the length of the fabric but half the width. Pin the interfacing to the wrong side of half the waistband, tack 1.5cm (⅝in) in from the edges and slip stitch to the centre. Turn up 1.5cm (⅝in) on the other long edge and press. For girls' trousers, place right sides together and pin the interfaced side of the waistband to the trousers extending the left hand side by 1.5cm (⅝in) and

the right end by 2.8cm (1⅛in) beyond the zip opening. Reverse this procedure for boys' trousers. Stitch into place taking a 1.5cm (⅝in) seam. Trim the interfacing close to the stitching-line and grade the seam allowances. Press the seam towards the waistband. Fold the waistband in half lengthwise with right sides together and sew the short sides taking a 1.5cm (⅝in) seam allowance. Clip the corners diagonally and grade the seam allowances. Turn the waistband to the right side and pull out the corners gently with a pin. Turn under 1.5cm (⅝in) on the remaining long edge and hem into place on the seamline. Press and close the waistband with hooks and eyes or snaps sewn under the overlap.

Trousers with an elastic casing obviously do not require a zip as they can easily be pulled on and off. This is

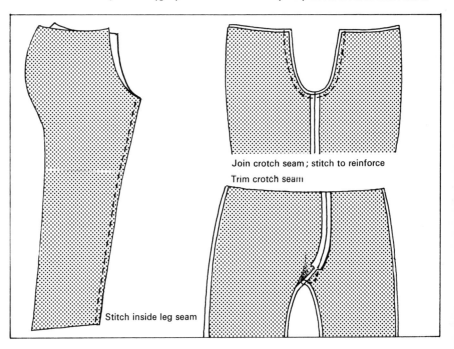

Join crotch seam; stitch to reinforce

Trim crotch seam

Stitch inside leg seam

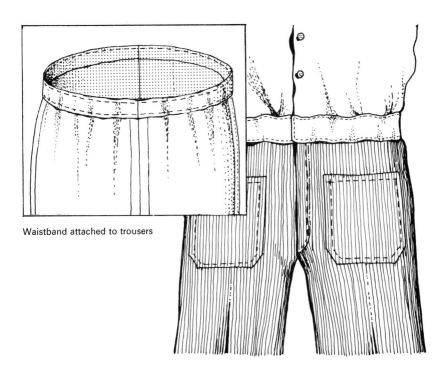

Waistband attached to trousers

another point in their favour when teaching your child to dress on his own as then he will not have to fiddle with awkward fastenings. If a zip is required this can be inserted either in the side seam, in the normal way, or in the centre front with a mock fly opening (see page 43).

When making up the trousers, first sew up the inside leg seam, press open and neaten. Match up the inside leg seams and join the crotch seam. Reinforce the curved part of the seam which goes between the legs, with a second row of stitching over the first extending a little way on either side. Trim this part of the seam to within 3mm ($\frac{1}{8}$in) of the reinforced stitching, and press open the remaining parts of the seam. Sew up the outside leg

seam last so any last-minute adjustments can be made and a zip can be inserted if required.

A very large hem would be too bulky for trousers, so a turn-up can be made which can easily be let down when the child begins to grow. Cut the trouser legs 10cm (4in) longer than the finished length. Neaten the raw edge and turn up the 10cm (4in) to the wrong side. Hem into place by hand and press on the lower edge. Turn up 5cm (2in) to the right side of the trousers and press. Catch stitch the underside of the turn-ups to the side seams to hold them in place.

Seam Finishes

It is most important, especially in children's clothes, that the inside of the garment is finished off neatly and the seams are as flat as possible so that there are no rough edges and bulky seams to rub and chafe delicate skins. As children's clothes spend a good deal of time in the washing machine, neatening edges will prolong their life by preventing the fabric from fraying until the seams disintegrate.

There are several ways of neatening seams but each one should be neatened as you go along. Do not wait until the garment is finished because it will be very difficult to neaten a seam completely once it is joined to another garment section. First press the seam open and then choose one of the following methods according to the weight of fabric being used and the amount it frays.

The simplest and quickest way for fabrics which do not fray is to trim the seam with pinking shears. This will give a notched edge to the fabric, but you must be careful to cut in a straight line to keep the seam even. If the fabric will fray only slightly, pinking shears can again be used, but first run a line of stitching 6mm ($\frac{1}{4}$in) in from the edge along the seam and then trim.

Fabrics which fray a great deal can be neatened either by hand or by machine. Set the machine to a small zig-zag stitch and sew close to the edge of the seam allowance. Neaten by hand with overcast stitches. First run a row of machine stitches or sew by hand with small running stitches along the seam 3mm ($\frac{1}{8}$in) in from the raw edge.

Oversew the raw edges with overcast stitches along the stitching-line at 6mm ($\frac{1}{4}$in) intervals. The edges can be neatened either on their own on an open seam or overcast together if the seam is to be pressed to one side.

On a seam which is to be pressed to one side, if the fabric is not prone to fraying, a double-stitched seam can be used by running a second row of stitches close to the original seam through both layers of fabric and then trimmed close to the second line of stitching. This is a very good finish for garments which are going to be washed frequently.

On fine delicate fabrics which fray easily, run a row of machine stitches or small running stitches by hand along the length of the seam 3mm ($\frac{1}{8}$in) in from the raw edge. Turn under the

Machine stitched and trimmed with pinking shears

Machine stitched with zig-zag

Seam finishes

Overcast by hand

fabric on the stitching-line to the wrong side and stitch again close to the folded edge.

For thick fabrics which fray and are too bulky to be turned under, such as wools, the edges can be blanket stitched by hand. Make a series of even, straight stitches and catch the working thread under the point of the needle so that it forms a loop which is pulled flat along the raw edge. These fabrics can also be neatened by binding the edges with bias binding. Fold the bias binding over both sides of the raw edge, encasing it in the binding, and machine or hand-stitch with small running stitches along the narrow side of the binding.

Neaten delicate transparent fabrics with a tiny rolled hem. Press both sides of the seam allowance together and trim to 1 cm ($\frac{3}{8}$in). With your fingers roll the edges together to the seamline so that the raw edges are encased. Sew into place with a whipping stitch keeping the stitches evenly spaced. Do not pull the thread too tightly as this will cause the seam to pucker.

The French seam is used on fine, delicate fabrics which fray and is especially common on blouses and lingerie which are in constant contact with the skin. Basically, it is a double seam with one seam encased inside another. Begin with the fabric's wrong sides together and make the first seam 1 cm ($\frac{3}{8}$in) in from the raw edges. Trim the seam to 3mm ($\frac{1}{8}$in) and press open. Turn the fabric over and with right sides together press flat at the seamline. Make a second seam 6mm ($\frac{1}{4}$in) in from the folded edge covering the raw edges of the first seam.

A final method of neatening on lightweight fabrics which fray is to bind one side of the seam allowance over the top of the other. Trim one side of the seam allowance to 3mm ($\frac{1}{8}$in). Stitch under 3mm ($\frac{1}{8}$in) on the raw edge of the other side and fold it over the top of the trimmed seam allowance and sew into place on the original seamline.

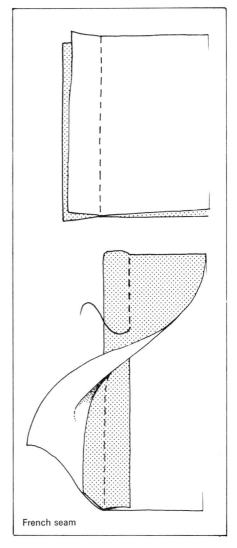

French seam

Making Clothes Last Longer

Simple Adjustments and Alterations

As children grow so quickly, clothing them can be quite a problem. If you make the clothes a size too big, your child is swamped until he grows into them and then it seems only two minutes before the clothes are too small. Easy adjustments can be made, as the child begins to grow, if simple allowances are included when the garment is first made up.

A very deep or double hem is ideal as mentioned in the sections on hems. On a waisted or empire-line dress, the adjustment can be made where the skirt is joined to the bodice. Lengthen the bodice allowance by approximately 5cm (2in), join the skirt in the correct position and leave the extra fabric on the inside. It can then be let down when required.

If you are lining a garment and have allowed extra length, do not forget to lengthen the lining as well so that both can be let down at the same time.

A good idea when constructing the garment is to make an inverted pleat at the sides or in the centre front. This is really a box pleat in reverse and is made on the wrong side of the fabric by turning two knife pleats away from each other. (Knife pleats are described in the section on pleats.) Not only does this sort of pleat have a slimming effect, but it will stretch as the child begins to grow and can be let out completely to give extra width to the garment.

Skirts and dresses can easily be lengthened by adding a pretty frill, either in the same fabric, if you have any left over, or in a contrasting band. Simply measure the width around the lower edge of the garment and note the amount by which you wish to lengthen it. Depending on the desired fullness of the frill, cut a straight piece of fabric either one and a half times or twice the length of the hem plus 3.2cm ($1\frac{1}{4}$in). To the depth required for lengthening add 3.2cm ($1\frac{1}{4}$in). If necessary, piece the fabric to give the required length. Neaten the raw edges. Fold the fabric in half lengthwise with right sides together and machine along the short side taking a 1.5cm ($\frac{5}{8}$in) seam. Press the seam open. Run two rows of gathering along one of the long edges and pull up the threads to the width around the lower edge of the garment. Having let down the existing hem, join to the gathered edge of the frill right sides together, taking a 1.5cm ($\frac{5}{8}$in) seam and distributing the gathers evenly. Press the seam up towards the main part of the garment. Turn up 1.5cm ($\frac{5}{8}$in) on the lower edge and hem stitch into place.

Trousers can also be lengthened in this way by cutting a piece of fabric the length of the bottom of the trouser leg plus 3.2cm ($1\frac{1}{4}$in) by the amount to be lengthened in depth plus 3.2cm ($1\frac{1}{4}$in). Neaten the raw edges. Fold the fabric strip in half lengthwise with right sides together and machine along the short side taking a 1.5cm ($\frac{5}{8}$in) seam. Press the seam open. Let down the existing hem on the trouser leg and join the fabric to the trousers right sides together taking a 1.5cm ($\frac{5}{8}$in) seam. Press the seam towards the original trouser leg. Turn up 1.5cm ($\frac{5}{8}$in) on the lower edge and hem stitch into place.

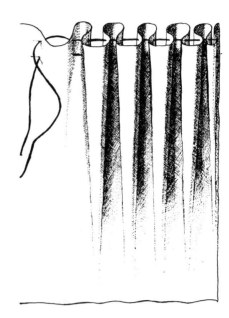

(*Right*) Insert two rows of gathering thread
(*Below left*) Inverted pleat
(*Below right*) Skirt lengthened by adding frill,
seen from wrong side

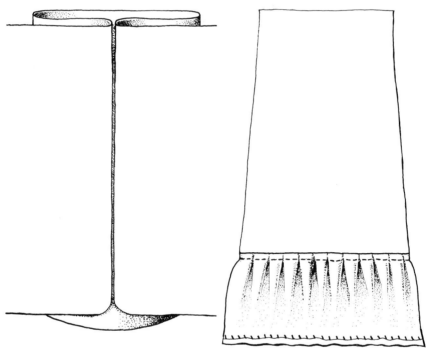

Making Clothes Last Longer

Another way to revitalise clothes which have become too short is to shorten them still further.

Trousers can be turned into 'plus twos'. Cut off the trouser legs 3.2cm (1¼in) below the knee. Neaten the raw edge and turn up 1.5cm (⅝in). Machine or hand sew with a continuous running stitch 3mm (⅛in) in from the edge to form a casing, leaving a 2.5cm (1in) opening. Measure the width around the child's leg and cut a piece of elastic this length plus 1.3cm (½in). Attach a safety pin to one end of the elastic and insert it through the casing. Overlap the ends of the elastic by 6mm (¼in) and sew them securely together. Stitch the gap in the casing.

You can also shorten a dress to prolong its life. Cut it to just below the waist plus 1.5cm (⅝in). Neaten the raw edge and turn up a 1.5cm (⅝in) hem. Tack and sew into place with tiny hemming stitches. Press and remove the tacking stitches. The dress can then be worn as a top with trousers or skirts.

Children's clothes which have become too tight can be let out by inserting godets into the side seams. A godet is a shaped piece of fabric which is inserted into a fitted garment to allow fullness from a given point. In a dress this can be used to give extra width across the chest, waist and hip and in a skirt to give extra width over the hip. Open up the side seams in the existing garment to just below the armhole or waistband. Cut out a triangular piece of fabric, grading to a point at the top, but remember to allow for a seam at either side and a hem at the bottom. Insert the godet, joining it to the original seams, neaten and press. Turn up the hem and sew into place. A godet can be made from the leftover fabric of the original garment or from a contrasting fabric provided it is compatible in weight otherwise it will pull the garment out of shape.

When a simple dress which is gathered on to a yoke becomes too short, it can be revitalised by turning it into a skirt. There are two ways of doing this but first remove the yoke. Then you can either adjust the gathers, pulling up or letting out as the case may be, to fit the child's waist comfortably. Undo the side seam and insert a zip. Join the gathered skirt to a waistband of self-fabric, if you have any left over, or of a contrasting fabric compatible in weight. Or you can let the

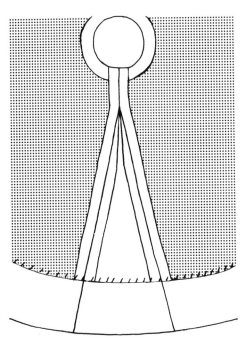

Godet in side seam

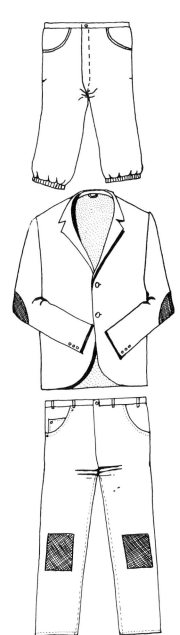

gathers out completely and turn the
top edge to the wrong side, machining
top and bottom to form a casing. Thread
the elastic through the casing to fit
your child's waist comfortably and
this will form a pretty, gathered skirt.

Mending

Children's clothes have to stand up to a
tremendous battering. When your
child is not busy growing out of them,
he will probably seem to delight in
wearing them out very quickly indeed.
He will go out to play or off to school
in brand new clothes, looking all spick
and span, and as if by magic, almost
overnight, holes and thin patches
appear. A stitch in time saves nine
may be an old adage, but darning and
patching play a very important part in
the life of children's clothes.

25

Darning and Patching

Darning

Small holes and patches which have become thin during wear can be repaired by darning. You will need a darning needle which stretches from one side of the darn to the other, with an eye large enough to thread the wool through without separating the strands. A darning mushroom is useful to insert under the material as this will ensure a flat darn. Use a slightly finer wool than that of the garment and for fabrics other than wool use the corresponding thread (eg cotton for cotton). To make the repair less noticeable, it is best to darn from the wrong side, but with garments, such as vests, worn next to the skin it is more comfortable if the darn is worked from the right side to avoid irritation.

In areas where the fabric has become thin but has not actually worn away into a hole, such as elbows, knees and heels, use a strengthening darn. The darning stitches must extend outside the weak part into the surrounding firm material, which will take the strain, and be worked evenly to retain elasticity. Start at the bottom left hand side just below the weak area, in the firm material, running the first line of stitching over and under the alternate fibres of the material in a vertical line and extend the stitches into the firm material at the top as well. Leave a tiny loop at the end of the row to allow for shrinkage during washing and to maintain elasticity. Repeat the stitching in the opposite direction but start one fibre higher so that the under loop of the first row becomes the upper of the

Darning

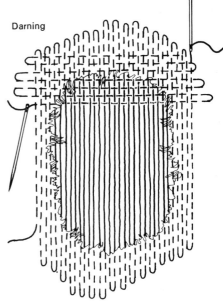

next and vice versa. Repeat these alternating rows extending into the firm material at each side of the darn. If an actual hole appears in the fabric or it is very thin, further rows of darning stitches will be necessary. These should go horizontally over and under the vertical lines already worked and be kept close together.

Patching

A patch should be used to repair an area which is too large to darn. It should be made from a fabric which is compatible with the original material to avoid pulling the outfit out of shape, and, unless used for decorative purposes, should be as invisible as possible. If the garment has faded slightly during wear, the fabric for the patch can be washed in a mild bleach so that it will tone in. When a printed fabric is used, try to match it up exactly with the design of the garment.

Cut a square or oblong, according to the shape of the hole, large enough to cover the gap and the weak fabric surrounding it. Turn in the edges of the patch by approximately 1 cm ($\frac{3}{8}$in) to the wrong side. Pin the patch to the right side of the garment, matching the fabric pattern, and tack into place. Remove the pins and hem or machine on the edge of the patch. Turn to the wrong side of the garment and trim the raw edges of the tear to 1 cm ($\frac{3}{8}$in) in from the sewing-line. Oversew the edges to neaten and prevent them fraying but do not catch up the fabric of the patch or the stitches will show through to the right side.

If the garment is made from a plain fabric, and there is no worry about matching up the design, the patch can be applied from the wrong side of the outfit. Prepare the patch as before. Pin, tack and sew the patch into position underneath the hole. On the right side turn in the raw edges of the tear and sew the folded edge to the patch with tiny hemming stitches.

Patches can now be fashionable and fun, so why not make them an obvious decorative feature by using a contrasting fabric. For instance, you can buy packs of pretty squares from Laura Ashley shops. Applying leather patches to jacket elbows or jersey elbows gives a grown-up look, which little boys will love. Also available is a wide range of novelty patches with motifs which can either be ironed on or sewn into place. A patch is quick and easy to apply with iron-on hemming web. Not only will hemming web save time, by sticking the patch into place, but it will also bond the ragged edges around the tear and prevent them from fraying. Patches can also be highlighted by hand-sewing them into place with a decorative blanket stitch in a contrasting, but not clashing, coloured thread.

When clothes are first made up, it can be a good idea to patch up areas which are going to be under the most strain, thus strengthening them to begin with.

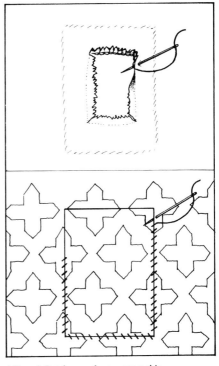

(*Above*) Patch seen from wrong side
(*Below*) Patch seen from right side

Patchwork

Patchwork takes a little time and patience but it is a great money-saver because patches can be made up from small pieces of left-over fabric. It is very enjoyable too, as you can give full vent to your creative flair and imagination. Matching is not really necessary unless you have a specific design or colour scheme in mind. Patches can be different shapes and sizes and the more fabric designs used the brighter and jollier the finished effect will be. It is a very pretty idea for simple children's wear such as skirts, tops and aprons and makes an attractive design for holdalls for shoes, laundry, toys, school books, pencils, crayons and paints. Patchwork is a lovely way, too, to brighten up the nursery in the form of cot covers or bedspreads and cushions. Packs of regular-shaped patches can be obtained from Laura Ashley shops which produce prints ideal for children's clothes.

There are really only two basic points to watch out for when making up patchwork. One is to ensure that the patches are of the same weight of cloth to avoid the patchwork being pulled out of shape, and the other is to avoid fabrics which fray easily otherwise the edges of each patch must be neatened first. Decide on the amount of material required and, as with quilting, make up the patchwork before cutting out each section.

Begin by tracing the patchwork shapes on to heavy card. Cut these out and use them as patterns from which to cut your patches. When cutting remember to leave a 6mm ($\frac{1}{4}$in)

seam allowance around each fabric shape, which will be required for joining the patches together. You will need a large, smooth surface on which to work. The floor is often the best place of all. It is easiest to work in long strips, stitching the patches together and pressing the seams open to keep the work flat. Join the strips together and press open the long seams. Continue joining the strips until you have sufficient area for the work you have planned. Pin the relevant pattern pieces to the fabric and cut as you would an ordinary fabric.

The fabric can be lined. This is particularly necessary with bedspreads and clothes worn next to the skin. Cut out the lining the same size as the patchwork plus a 1.5cm ($\frac{5}{8}$in) seam allowance. With right sides together machine around three sides, taking a 1.5cm ($\frac{5}{8}$in) seam. Trim the seam, cut corners diagonally and clip curves. Turn through to the right side of the fabric and turn in the seam allowance. Then catch stitch the opening on the fourth side together.

If you are making patchwork cushions it may be a good idea to insert a zip, or two strips of self-adhesive fabric, into one of the seam allowances so that the cushion can easily be removed before washing or dry cleaning the patchwork.

Patchwork quilts also look most attractive in children's bedrooms. Just make up the amount of patchwork to cover the area required and use it as the top fabric. It can be quilted in the same way as a regular fabric (for directions see the section on quilting).

(*Right*) Join patches together in a strip;
Join strips together
(*Below*) Finished patchwork quilt

29

Fur and Synthetic Fabrics

Fur

There is a wide and exciting variety of fake furs on the market suitable for children's jackets, coats, caps and mittens. They are fun to wear as well as a good way to keep warm and snug in winter. The fabric can also be used for making up soft toys such as teddy bears and other toy characters, like The Wombles, which are produced by pattern manufacturers but which are so expensive to buy ready-made. Fake fur is not nearly as difficult to work with as many people imagine provided a few golden rules are remembered.

Fur is a with nap fabric and the pile goes in one direction, so you must ensure that all the pattern pieces are laid out the same way, with the pile of the fur going down towards the hem. Place the pattern pieces out singly on the wrong side of the fabric and mark the shapes with tailor's chalk. Obviously, because of the bulk of the fabric, it would be difficult to place a pattern piece to a fold. Instead, lay out the pattern piece and pin along the foldline with the pins parallel to this line. Mark around the tissue, turn exactly on the pinline and mark the other half of the garment section. Cut out each pattern piece individually with a sharp razor blade or the point of very sharp scissors. Be careful to cut the backing only, which will help prevent the fur from shedding.

As the fabric is so thick, it would be very difficult to tack sections together. The pieces should be pinned to each other at 1.3cm ($\frac{1}{2}$in) intervals, with the pins going horizontally across the seam to ensure that there is no movement under the machine. Before beginning to sew, comb the fur away from the seam edges. However, if some strands become caught in the seam, pull them out gently on the right side with a pin. It is important always to use a synthetic thread and if you are using a machine set it for a medium length stitch. To be certain that you have the correct stitch length and tension setting, it is a good idea to test on a small sample of the fabric before finally machining.

Synthetic Fabrics

Synthetic fabrics tend to collect a great deal of static electricity and it may help if you wash the material in an anti-static conditioner before making up in order to avoid the fabric clinging in the wrong places causing the seams to pucker. For knitted

Fur jacket

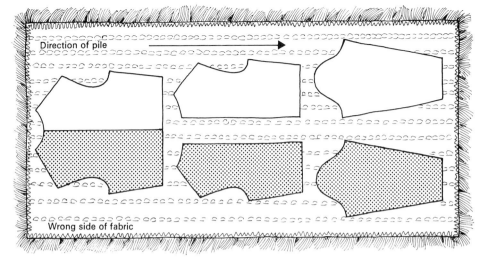

'With nap' layout for fur jacket

synthetic fabrics, use a ball-point needle which will go between the fibres of the material and prevent snagging or tearing. Some synthetics are likely to ladder in one direction and this should be checked by gently pulling the cut edge. If laddering occurs, ensure that the pattern pieces are laid out with the laddered edge to the hem and strengthen the raw edge with a machine zig-zag stitch. With very stretchy fabrics, tissue paper can be tacked to the underside of the seam. This will help to hold the shape and it can easily be torn away after machining. If the fabric is very slippery, tissue paper can be inserted into the seam, between the two layers of fabric, and again it can easily be torn away after stitching.

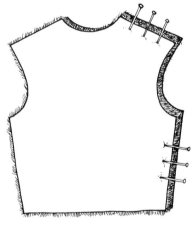

Pin seams at 1.3cm ($\frac{1}{2}$in) intervals with pins at right angles to seams

31

Quilting

Anoraks and quilted jackets are expensive to buy and even ready-quilted fabric is quite costly in the shops. However, it is quite simple to quilt your own. Quilting is just the stitching together of two layers of fabric with a layer of filler between them. It should be remembered that the fabric must be quilted before cutting out your garment.

Firstly, lay out your pattern pieces on the fabric to ensure that you have a rectangle of fabric with 5cm (2in) to spare around the edges, which will be taken up as the fabric is quilted. Remove the pattern pieces and press the fabric flat. Cut a rectangle of the filler the same size using either polyester or cotton wadding 28g (1oz) in weight or, for a lighter padding, use one or two layers of flannelette or non-woven interlining. Cut a further rectangle of very light-weight batiste for the backing and press flat.

Mark the quilting lines diagonally on the outside of the fabric with sharpened tailor's chalk, beginning across one corner and continue to mark the diagonal lines 3.2cm (1¼in) apart. Then repeat the procedure from the opposite direction.

Place the filler on top of the backing and then put the top fabric over the filler, with the outside of the fabric uppermost, and pin the three layers together. Tack the layers together by hand with large stitches, working diagonally from corner to corner, starting from the centre and sewing towards the edges to prevent the fabric from slipping. Leave the pins in place.

The fabric is now ready for quilting. To ensure the stitch length and tension are correct, first practise stitching on a test sample of the three layers. Then with the tension press adjusted and the stitch length set, start from a centre marking line and stitch slowly from one edge to the other, guiding the fabric in front and behind the sewing foot to smooth the fabric outwards away from the foot. Stitch the rows in alternate directions to keep the fabric in place. Work very slowly when crossing previous rows, stretching the fabric slightly to avoid puckering ; and prevent the fabric from hanging off the back of the machine. If necessary, cut the tacking threads while stitching is in progress in order to keep the fabric smooth. When the whole piece is quilted ensure that all the tacking threads are removed.

The pattern pieces can now be laid out and cut in the normal way. After sewing sections together, remove the

Marking quilting lines

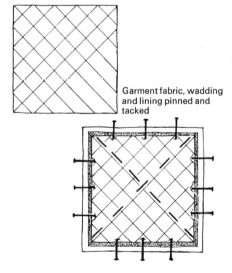

Garment fabric, wadding and lining pinned and tacked

wadding from the seam allowances to avoid bulky seams. When pressing use a steam iron to prevent the quilting becoming flattened.

Remnants

The remnant counter provides many bargains ideal for children's clothes because their small, simple outfits rarely take more than 1.20m (1¼yd) of 90cm (36in) wide fabric and frequently use up less. You may find as well that a child's garment can be made out of fabric left over from your own clothes, especially if you lay the two patterns out together and intersperse the pattern pieces.

A favoured look today is to make up an outfit in more than one fabric, teaming up prints and plains, combining two or even three prints together, and co-ordinating matching large and small prints. This is a marvellous way to use up small pieces of fabric by making them into contrasting yokes, collars, cuffs,

pockets or frills, all of which can look most effective.

In fact, there are many ways in which remnants can be useful, pretty and money-saving at the same time. Use them to make up hats, caps, mittens, bibs or purses ; or make them into attractive bags to hold toys, shoes, laundry, nightdresses, pencils and paints, thus encouraging your child to be tidy. And they are perfect for dolls' clothes.

Sew along quilting lines

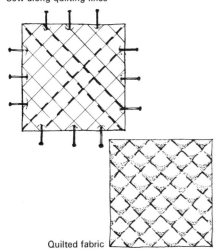

Quilted fabric

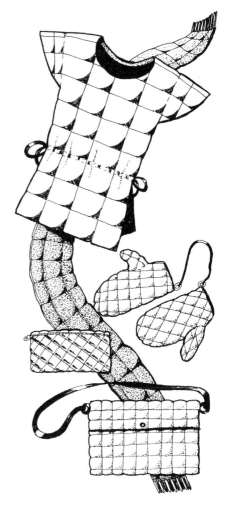

Decorative Finishes

Decorative embroidery, trimmings, appliqué and iron-on transfers greatly enhance the prettiness of children's clothes, especially when used on plain fabrics. But when they are already included on ready-to-wear clothes they usually send the high price still higher. However, the stitches are basically simple and can easily be done by hand, with a little time and patience, if you are not lucky enough to own one of those marvellous modern sewing machines which will do the work for you.

Decorative Embroidery

Elaborate embroidery would be too heavy and fussy for children's clothes so choose simple motifs and designs. Freestyle embroidery is probably the most popular and commonly used for children's clothes, the stitches being worked over an iron-on or traced transfer. Many paper patterns include iron-on transfers for embroidery and a

selection of transfers can be bought from specialist needlework shops. If you wish to be more creative you can trace your own design.

For embroidering, you will need a crewel needle for fine and medium-weight threads and fabrics, and a chenille needle for heavier weights ; a sharp pair of scissors with pointed blades, and a thimble to protect your middle finger when working. There are various types of embroidery thread to choose from according to the type of design and fabric being used. It is important, though, to use a yarn which is compatible with the fabric. Stranded embroidery cotton is very useful as the strands can be separated and used either singly or in groups depending on the desired effect. An embroidery ring may be needed, to keep the fabric smooth and taut, if you are using closely-worked stitches which might pucker.

Transfers

Iron-on transfer designs are generally impressed on the fabric by placing the transfer face down on the fabric and applying a hot iron for a few seconds to release the ink. The backing paper can then be gently pulled away. However, the manufacturers' instructions should be followed closely as they can vary.

Home Designing

There are several ways to impress a tracing of your own design on to a fabric. The easiest way to trace is to use carbon paper—yellow or light blue for dark fabrics and black or dark blue on light-coloured fabrics. Place the carbon paper face down on the fabric,

then put the drawing or tracing of the design on top and secure in place. Take a pencil with a sharp point and draw over the lines being careful to press only on the design lines or the carbon may smudge the fabric. Remove the carbon and drawing and place a sheet of tissue paper over the impression on the fabric. Press with a warm iron to fix the design on to the fabric and prevent the colour from coming off on the embroidery threads.

Another method is to trace the design on to firm tracing paper. Mark the lines of the design with a needle, pricking small holes about 1.5mm ($\frac{1}{16}$in) apart. Remove any roughness from the back of the design by rubbing it with fine sandpaper. Place the design on to the fabric, using weights to keep it in place. Rub french chalk for dark fabrics and powdered charcoal on light colours through the holes. Take the tracing off and blow away any surplus powder. Then paint over the dotted lines with water colour, using dark or light paint depending on the colour of the material.

With fine transparent fabrics, such as nylon or voile, the design can be traced directly on to the material. Place the design under the material and hold firmly in position. Trace with a soft pencil or water-colour paint and then iron the impression under a piece of tissue paper to prevent the colour from coming off on to the embroidery threads.

Embroidery Stitches

Embroidery stitches are generally worked from left to right. There are many, many embroidery stitches and there are lots of publications giving an in-depth study of the subject. Described below are some basic stitches which are easy to do and their simplicity of design makes them ideal for children's clothes. They look just as attractive when used on their own, or combined as part of an overall design.

Stem Stitch

This is basically an outline stitch and can be used singly for flower stems or can be made to fill in a shape by working rows of the stitch close together. Take even, slightly slanting stitches over the outline and work from left to right with the thread coming out on the left-hand side of the previous stitch.

Running Stitch

This stitch is easily recognisable from everyday sewing, but ensure that the top stitches are of equal length and the under stitches about half the length of the upper ones. This stitch can be used very effectively as a border around the bottom of skirts, dresses and jackets by looping a contrasting coloured thread through the upper stitches, but do be careful not to catch the fabric.

Scroll Stitch

This can make a very pretty border. Again working from left to right, loop the thread to the right and then back to the left on the fabric. Take a small slanting stitch to the left under the line of the design inside the loop and pull

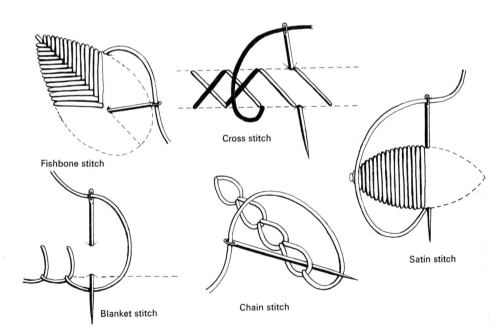

Fishbone stitch

Cross stitch

Blanket stitch

Chain stitch

Satin stitch

the thread through over the top of the loop. Space the stitches evenly.

Straight Stitch

These stitches are the basis for several different designs. They can be used as a series of single, regular stitches spaced out to give a shape or they can vary in size. If the straight stitches are worked closely together covering a shape, they are known as satin stitch. A large or irregular shape can be filled with straight stitches of varying sizes known as long and short stitch. If a shaded effect is desired, alternate long and short stitches around the outline of the shape and then work the filling rows of stitches to give a smooth look.

Fishbone Stitch

This is useful for filling small shapes such as leaves. Take a small straight stitch along the centreline of the shape and end with the needle on the left hand side of the stitch. Take a sloping stitch to the centre at the foot of the first stitch. Make a similar sloping stitch from the right hand side of the first stitch just below the first sloping stitch so that it overlaps at the centreline and continue working from alternate sides until the space is filled with overlapping sloping stitches.

Cross Stitch

This is very easy and attractive. Make a series of sloping stitches from left to right keeping them the same length and equidistant. Then repeat the stitches from the opposite direction to form the cross.

Blanket Stitch

This is often used as a decorative form of top stitching to attach patches and appliqués and it is equally useful for neatening raw edges. Make a straight stitch vertically and repeat with even stitches catching the working thread under the needle as it emerges at the top to form a loop. Pull the thread up so that the loop is level either with the edge of the fabric or with the top of the stitches if it is being used as a border.

Chain Stitch

This is another basic stitch upon which other designs are formed. Hold the thread where it emerges with the left thumb and make a small loop returning the needle to this spot and insert again bringing it out at a short distance ahead with the loop under the needle. Repeat and the stitch will form a chain. Lazy daisy stitch is worked in the same manner, but the head of the loop is secured with a small stitch.

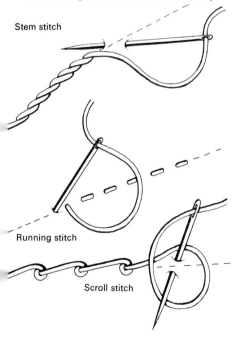

Stem stitch

Running stitch

Scroll stitch

Trimmings

Gaily-coloured braids, ribbons, rick-rack and lace give a pretty finishing touch to children's clothes. Children are easily bored with clothes and adding trimmings is a good way to give clothes a different look and a new lease of life.

Soutache and other narrow braids are attached with a single row of stitching either by hand, or by machine using a braiding foot. Test on a sample of the fabric first and, if the braid begins to pucker, place tissue paper under the fabric before machining. This paper is easily torn away after the stitching is completed.

With wider, flat braids both edges have to be stitched into place. Stitch around the outside edge first and then along the inner edge. Some trimmings can be damaged by machine stitching, so test first. If the trimmings are unsuitable for machining, they should be applied by hand using a back stitch. To ensure a smooth, flat finish when going around a square corner, it is necessary to mitre the trimming. Stitch on the outside edge to the point of the corner, then back stitch and clip the threads. The loose end of the trimming is folded back over the stitched part. Note the width of the trimming and transfer this measurement to the inside of the stitching-line, marking the point with tailor's chalk on the trimming. Stitch diagonally from the corner to this point, then press. Pull down the free end of the trimming and it will go neatly around the corner. Press again and continue to stitch the rest of the outside edge. Complete

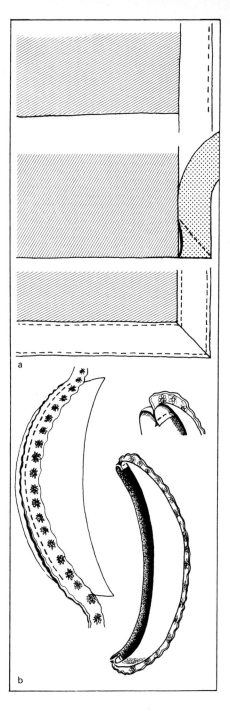

a

b

by sewing along the inside edge.

Rick-rack makes a pretty piping and an attractive edging on an outfit. When used as a piping first turn under the edge of the fabric to the wrong side and press. Lap the folded edge over the rick-rack to the centre of the trimming, covering half of it. Stitch very close to the edge of the fabric, exposing the remainder of the rick-rack to form the piping. When used as an edging both sides of the rick-rack show. Fold under the seam allowance of the fabric to the wrong side and press. Position the rick-rack on the right side of the fabric with the centre of the trimming to the foldline. Stitch along the foldline through the centre of the rick-rack. Bands of rick-rack in one or more colours can also be used to form a decorative border around the bottom of skirts. To ensure the trimming is level, first mark the position of the bands using a measure and tailor's chalk. Measure the length required plus 6mm ($\frac{1}{4}$in). Turn under each end of the trimming by 3mm ($\frac{1}{8}$in) to neaten. Place the rick-rack over the chalk mark and stitch through the centre of the trimming.

Lace makes a very dainty trimming and small amounts can turn a simple style into a pretty dress for parties. You can even make your child's christening robe or bridesmaid's dress. Choose a narrow, fine lace with a small design for collars, cuffs and pockets. A wider lace may be used around the bottom of a dress. Wide, coarser lace is a perfect way to lengthen a cotton skirt giving it a pretty, peasant look.

Lace can be sewn by hand or machine, but a fine thread and fine, sharp needle must be used in order to make the stitching line as inconspicuous as possible. If you wish to have a gathered lace edging, this can either be bought pre-gathered, or you can gather it yourself by pulling up a thread in the upper edge to the required amount of fullness. Secure the end of the thread by winding it around a pin and adjust the gathers evenly.

When attaching lace trimming to the bottom of a dress or skirt, pin the right side of the lace to the right side of the finished hem, keeping the edges of the lace and the hem level with each other. Sew the two together with small whipping stitches. When joining the lace by machine, put the wrong side of the lace to the right side of the fabric with the edge of the lace 3mm ($\frac{1}{8}$in) above the hem. Machine along the edge of the lace using a zig-zag stitch.

Use gathered lace trimming for collars and cuffs, inserting the lace between the top and the facing. Pin and tack the straight edge of the lace to the right side of the collar and cuff over the seamline and, if possible, level with the raw edge of the fabric. If the lace is too narrow move it slightly closer to the seamline. On a collar, taper the ends of the lace so that they do not overlap when the garment is worn. With the ruffled edge of the lace towards the centre of the collar or cuff, pin to the facing, right sides together, tack, remove pins and machine on the seamline. Trim the seam, clip curves and cut corners diagonally. Turn the section through to the right side showing the lace edging.

(a) Trimming a square corner
(b) Attaching lace trimming to a collar

Appliqué

Appliqués are fun and make a cheap and cheerful way to brighten up children's clothes. Motifs can be added to pockets, collars and around the hem to form a decorative border. You can buy appliqué patterns or trace your own designs. Appliqués can even be made from scraps of left-over fabric. One or more fabrics may be used for highlighting features in the design, such as eyes on an animal motif or flower stems and petals. Felt is an ideal fabric to use as it does not fray so the edges don't have to be neatened. So, when working with this fabric, ignore the following references to seam allowances as they are totally unnecessary.

Appliqué can be done by hand or machine. If working by hand, stitch around the outline of the design. Cut out the shape, leaving a 3mm ($\frac{1}{8}$in) seam allowance outside the row of stitching. Turn under the edges to the wrong side on the stitching-line, tack and press. Pin the appliqué into position and attach, using a decorative blanket stitch or hemming stitch. Remove the pins and the tacking thread. The appliqué can also be machined into place stitching on the edge instead of hand-sewing.

In general, when applied by machine, allow a 6mm ($\frac{1}{4}$in) seam allowance around the edges. Pin or tack the motif into position and machine stitch on the seamline. Trim the fabric close to the row of stitching and machine the raw edges with a very small zig-zag stitch. For extra interest, the appliqués can be applied with brightly coloured or contrasting threads.

There are two quick and easy short-cuts to appliqué. The first of these is to buy some of the very attractive four-colour iron-on transfers featuring a variety of motifs, initials and embroidery. These are easy to apply by simply placing the transfer face down on the fabric and pressing with a hot iron. The transfer is left to cool and the backing paper removed. However, it is essential that the manufacturer's instructions are followed carefully as they can vary. Also check that your fabric is suitable and will not shrivel up under the heat of the iron. Alternatively, you can apply your own motifs by inserting a strip of hemming web between the appliqué

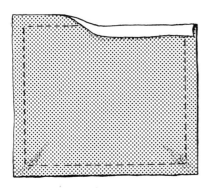

and the fabric and ironing into place. Appliqués are not only decorative in their own right, but they also make very useful and attractive patches for covering holes or thin, worn material.

Decorative zips are great fun on children's clothes as they are sewn on the outside of the garment and act as attractive trimmings. Machine the seam to the bottom of the zip and tack

(*Opposite*) Turn edge of fabric under
Sew into place with blanket stitch

up the remainder of the opening on the seamline. Press the seam open. On the outside of the garment place the zip face up with the centre of the teeth over the seamline and the top of the zip 2.2cm ($\frac{7}{8}$in) below the top edge of the garment. Tack into position and turn under the raw edges of the tape at the bottom of the zip, to face the fabric. Sew by hand or machine, using a zipper foot, close to the teeth. Remove the tacking and press. Sew again down the outside edge of the zip.

Zips

Zips are easy to put in provided that a few golden rules are followed. They can be inserted either by hand or by machine, but if a machine is used a zipper foot will be necessary. Zips should always be put in by hand when using fabrics with a pile or nap so that the surface of the material is not distorted. It is also better not to machine them in if working with slippery materials, very fine delicate fabrics or knits which may pucker. Check that you have the correct length of zip. A child's measurements may be fine for the pattern size for the chest, waist and hips but if he is shorter in height the zip opening might need to be shorter too. If possible, insert the zip into the garment section before the outfit is completed as it will be easier to handle.

There are several methods of putting in a zip. The easiest method is the one where the two sides of the opening meet together over the centre of the zip. Machine the seam to the bottom of the opening. Tack up the remainder of the seam and press the whole seam open. On the wrong side of the fabric, centre the zip over the opening, face downwards towards the seam, with the zip head 2.5cm (1in) below the top edge of the outfit. Tack the zip into place down both sides. Turn to the right side of the fabric and hand-stitch or machine with a zipper foot 6mm ($\frac{1}{4}$in) from the edge of the opening down one side, across the bottom of the zip, and up the other side. Press and remove the tacking stitches.

Separating zips are a marvellous way to fasten children's jackets, coats, tops and skirts. Children can operate them easily on their own so that they can quickly dress themselves instead of tussling with awkward buttons and having to wait for their mother to give them a helping hand. Turn under the seam allowance or facing on the foldline down either side of the opening, tack and press. With the zip closed, pin the right side of the zip to the wrong side of the opening, the edges meeting over the centre of the zip teeth. Open the zip and tack each side into place, turning in the tabs at

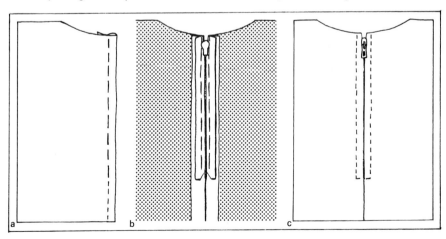

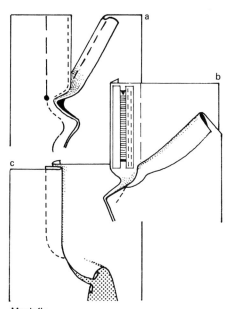

Mock fly
(a) Front seams extended; (b) Apply zip to left fly front; (c) Right front lapped over left and stitched

the top of the zip to face the fabric. Turn to the right side of the fabric and sew by hand with continuous running stitches or by machine using a zipper foot 6mm ($\frac{1}{4}$in) from the opening edges, catching in the tabs. Remove the tacking stitches and press.

Young boys love to feel grown-up and have clothes just like daddy's. In trousers, zips can be inserted down the centre front to give a mock fly opening. Extend the centre front seams by 2.5cm (1in) from the top of the opening to 5cm (2in) below the bottom of the zip, marking the centre fronts with tacking stitches or tailor's chalk. Put the zip with the slide 2.2cm ($\frac{7}{8}$in) below the seam allowance on the waist and mark the position of the

(*Opposite*) (a) Seam machined and tacked
(b) Zip tacked to inside (c) Zip stitched into place

zipper top stop. Remove the zip and stitch up the centre front seam from the marking finishing 3.8cm (1$\frac{1}{2}$in) away from the edge of the inside leg. Neaten the extension edge on the left front by stitching 6mm ($\frac{1}{4}$in) from the edge tapering the stitches towards the bottom. Turn the fabric under to the wrong side on the stitching-line and edge stitch in place. With the zip closed, pin it to the left, front face upwards, having the outside edge of the right zip tape 1cm ($\frac{3}{8}$in) inside the raw edge and the slide 2.2cm ($\frac{7}{8}$in) down from the top edge. Machine stitch using a zipper foot close to the outside edge of the left tape and place a second row of stitching 6mm ($\frac{1}{4}$in) inside this. Still keeping the zip closed, pin it to the right front with the outer edge of the tape 1cm ($\frac{3}{8}$in) inside the raw edge. Stitch into place close to the outer edge of the tape and again 6mm ($\frac{1}{4}$in) in from this stitching-line. Clip diagonally across the left front to the bottom of the zip. On the right side of the garment turn under the right front on the centre front marking, tack into place and press. Match up the centre fronts with the right front overlapping the left. Tack along the line 2.5cm (1in) inside the folded edge through all the layers curving the stitching at the bottom towards the crotch, but be careful not to catch in the extension on the left front. Machine along the line of tacking on the right side only and remove the tacking stitches. Turn over to the inside of the garment and catch stitch the lower edges of the front extensions together. Join to the waistband in the normal way, matching up the ends with the folded edges of the fly front extensions.

Buttons and Fastenings

Buttons should be chosen with care so that they add a decorative finishing touch to a garment apart from their obvious practical use as a fastening. Tiny round pearl buttoms and loops give a dainty look to a small girl's blouse or dress and, when used on a boy's shirt, turn it into a perfect pageboy's outfit. Brightly coloured and novelty buttons with motifs give a young look, ideal for children's clothes. Pick out one of the colours in a patterned fabric or choose a contrasting colour for the buttons and top stitching thread on plain materials. Metallic buttons on a blazer and mock leather buttons on a tweed coat or jacket look very smart and make the child feel very grown-up to have an outfit just like his parent's.

If you wish the buttons to match the material, but have difficulty in matching the colour, button trims covered with self-fabric are the answer. These come in various shapes and sizes and different weights : either metal for heavier fabrics or plastic for lightweight materials. The latter are perfect for children's clothes as they will not rust when subjected to constant washing. Covered buttons need not look old and fuddy-duddy either if you choose ones with decorative rims.

Snap fasteners and button trims with snaps underneath help to make a quick and easy-to-fasten outfit for busy mothers who haven't the time to spare for working buttonholes.
Manufacturers now produce these in different sizes with a very modern and young look and include some super metal ones which give an authentic look to denim outfits.
Another quick fastening method makes use of decorative zips, which are sewn on the outside of the garment, becoming an attractive feature of the outfit while avoiding time-consuming buttonholes.

Velcro, which is a self-adhesive fastening, can also be used in place of zips and buttons. Simply sew two strips to either side of the opening, press together to close and pull apart to open. Snaps, zips and Velcro, which are so easy to open and close, are also ideal fastenings for teaching children to dress themselves. Small fingers may find buttons fiddly and difficult to fasten and need their mother's help.

If you want buttonholes, they can be made either by hand or by machine. A quick way to fasten buttons, if you do not have a machine, is to make loops instead of buttonholes. The loops can be self-fabric made into a rouleau strip or they can be made from purchased cording or soutache braid. To make a self-fabric loop, cut a piece of material on the bias twice the finished width of the loop plus 1.3cm ($\frac{1}{2}$in) seam allowance. With the right sides together, fold the material in half lengthwise and machine along the long edge taking a 6mm ($\frac{1}{4}$in) seam. Trim very close to the stitching. Attach a strong thread to one end and insert through a darning needle. Turn the tube through to the right side with the aid of the needle and press. Cut the strip into loops so that they fit comfortably over the button and allow a seam allowance. Oversew the raw edges to neaten. Tack into position on

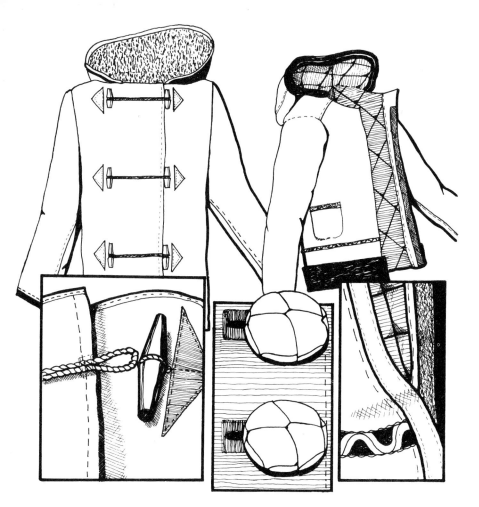

the right side of the garment. Join the facing to the garment over the top of the loops, right sides together, so that when the facing is turned through to the wrong side, the ends of the loops are encased. If you have insufficient self-fabric to make the loops, they

can be worked using buttonhole twist or silk thread. Attach two or three strands of thread close to the edge of the fabric opening, forming a loop large enough to slide comfortably over the button. Bind the strands together using a buttonhole stitch.

Buttonholes

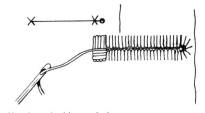

Hand-worked buttonhole

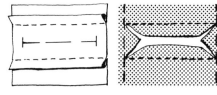

Bound buttonhole

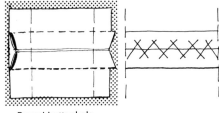

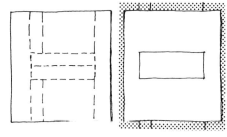

Faced buttonhole

Three methods of making buttonholes

To make a buttonhole by hand, first position the button on the fabric half its diameter in from the edge of the opening and mark the width of the button at either side. Make an eyelet hole with a stiletto at the end of the buttonhole, nearest the opening edge, which will hold the shank of the button. Allow approximately 3mm ($\frac{1}{8}$in) ease for the button to slide through comfortably. Using sharp, pointed scissors cut a slit to the inside mark to form the opening. Overcast the edges or sew, with continuous running stitches, around the opening to strengthen. Working from right to left sew with buttonhole stitches using buttonhole twist. These stitches are basically blanket stitches worked very closely together. The opposite end to the eyelet should be finished off with a bar tack. Make a few vertical straight stitches the width of the buttonhole and surrounding buttonhole stitches and bind these together. When a very strong buttonhole is required, as on coats and jackets, work the buttonhole stitches over a cord.

A bound buttonhole takes a little more time and patience but gives a neat finish and stands up well to wear and tear. There are several ways to make this sort of buttonhole. One method is to use a fabric patch, turned through to the inside. Cut a piece of fabric on the lengthwise grain 2.5cm (1in) longer than the width of the buttonhole by 3.8cm (1$\frac{1}{2}$in), and mark the centre of the patch with a row of tacking stitches. Fold one edge of the patch 6mm ($\frac{1}{4}$in) from the centre mark and tack on the foldline. Sew a tuck 3mm ($\frac{1}{8}$in) from the folded edge and remove the tacking. Repeat this procedure on the other side of the centreline so there is a 6mm ($\frac{1}{4}$in) space between the stitching-lines of the tucks. With right sides together centre the patch over the buttonhole position on the garment matching the centre tacking-line on the patch with the buttonhole marking. Tack the tucked piece to the main fabric along the centreline of tacking. Mark the ends of the buttonhole with tailor's chalk and sew along the stitching-lines on the tucks between these points. Cut a 6mm ($\frac{1}{4}$in) slit on the centreline of the buttonhole on the inside of the garment and then cut diagonally into each corner. Turn the tucked piece to the inside through the opening. Turn the garment over to the right side and fold the front edge back over the buttonhole exposing the triangular ends. Sew these ends to the tucks across the strip on the chalk marks indicating the ends of the buttonhole. Catch stitch the edges of the tucks together on the outside and cut the corners of the patch in a curve. Press the buttonhole from the inside. Join the facing and tack around each buttonhole to hold it securely in position. Mark the corners and centre of the buttonhole with pins and cut the facing as for the buttonhole opening, making a horizontal slit at the centre pin. Cut diagonally from the slit to the corners and turn in the edges to the facing. Sew to the stitching-line with very small hemming stitches. Remove the tacking and catch stitching and press. The buttonhole will now be the same on both sides.

Thick, bulky fabrics have to be fastened with a faced buttonhole and strengthened with fine cord. Cut a piece of fabric 3.8cm (1$\frac{1}{2}$in) larger all round than the size of the buttonhole and mark the centreline as before. With right sides together, centre the patch over the buttonhole marking on the garment, and tack into place. On the wrong side stitch around the buttonhole 3mm ($\frac{1}{8}$in) from the edge. Cut a 6mm ($\frac{1}{4}$in) slit on the centreline and cut diagonally into the corners. Turn the strip through the opening to the wrong side and press. Cut out two pieces of fabric 3.2cm (1$\frac{1}{4}$in) wide and fold each over fine cord 2.5cm (1in) longer than the buttonhole, stitching into place close to the cord. Sew these pieces together leaving a space in the centre the same size as the buttonhole. Centre the strips under the faced opening in the garments. Slip stitch the edges of the opening to the stitching-lines and across the ends of the corded strip, pulling the stitches tight so that they disappear into the fabric. Join the facing as before.

Buttons should be sewn into place using double strands of strong thread or buttonhole twist. If the button is not manufactured with a metal shank, a thread one can be formed while sewing the button into place. Anchor the thread on the wrong side of the fabric and take one stitch through the button. Insert a thick pin or matchstick under this stitch and continue to sew over the top. When completed, remove the pin or matchstick and pull the button to tighten the threads. Wind the thread around the strands under the button several times to form a shank. Secure the thread on the wrong side. The button can be attached by sewing through another small button on the inside of the fabric.

Gathering and Shirring

Gathering, shirring, smocking, tucking and pleating are all decorative ways of controlling fullness. Not only do they look very pretty on children's clothes but they are very practical as their elastic properties enable the clothes to stretch as the child begins to grow.

Gathering

Gathering is one of the most popular and simple ways to control fullness. It is used on lightweight materials including very fine wools. Gathering stitches must be even. When seams must be crossed, clip the seam allowance first so that the stitches can go between the clipped edges. The amount of fabric to be gathered

Gathering

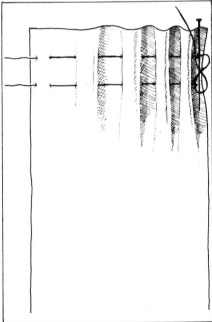

should be about one and a half times the finished width of an outfit—or twice the finished width if you prefer a very full garment.

The quickest and easiest way to gather is by machine. Wind the bobbin with thick thread or buttonhole twist and use a regular thread on top of the machine. Set the machine to the longest stitch and sew the first row of stitching on the seamline, leaving a long thread at each end of the row. Machine a second row of stitching 6mm ($\frac{1}{4}$in) inside the seamline, again leaving long threads at either end. Secure the threads firmly at one end, winding them around a pin. From the other end pull up the bobbin threads to the required width, and secure. Adjust the gathers evenly. To give a neat, flat finish to the gathers, stroke them down with a large needle, such as a darning needle, above and below the gathering threads about 1.3cm ($\frac{1}{2}$in) each way, taking care not to snag the fabric.

To gather by hand, make two rows of small running stitches, one under the other. The stitches must be perfectly even and the best way to do this is to make the stitches on the right side twice the size of the stitches on the under side. Anchor the thread at the beginning of the row with a series of small back stitches and continue with the running stitches to the far end. Pull up the thread to the required width and secure with back stitches. Adjust the gathers evenly. However, if the fabric is too delicate for stroking, make the rows of gathering wider apart, leaving about 6mm ($\frac{1}{4}$in) between them.

Gathering up a long length of

fabric can be a bit of a problem. It is difficult to get the gathers even, if they are all together. The best way is to divide the fabric to be gathered into four sections and then divide the rest of the garment to which it will be joined into quarters as well. Gather the four sections separately and pin to the corresponding quarter of the garment fabric. Pull up the gathering threads to fit, and adjust the gathers evenly.

Shirring

Shirring is the use of three or more rows of gathers to control fullness. A regular thread can be used and pulled up, as in gathering, but for children's clothes it is better to use thin elastic which will give extra stretch to allow for growth.

Only use the elastic thread on the bobbin, either by winding the bobbin

Shirring

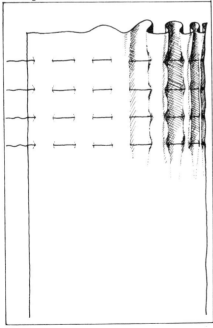

by hand without stretching the thread or by machine without using tension. Use the correct thread compatible with the fabric on top of the machine and a medium-size needle. Set the machine to the longest stitch length and test on a sample piece of the fabric to ascertain the correct amount of fullness. Machine in straight lines keeping the rows equidistant, about 6mm ($\frac{1}{4}$in) apart. It is important to stretch the fabric flat for each row of stitching. Therefore, if a large area such as a bodice, is to be shirred, the fabric must be worked before the garment section is cut out. Press with the tip of the iron only, being careful not to place the iron flat over the fullness as this would destroy the raised effect.

Smocking and Tucking

Smocking

Smocking looks most attractive on small children's clothes. The actual stitch is easy but great care must be taken in preparing the fabric first. The best materials to use are small checks, such as gingham, or narrow stripes, which will act as guidelines. With plain fabrics, the guidelines must be marked out with small dots, evenly spaced at approximately 6mm ($\frac{1}{4}$in) intervals in absolutely straight lines. Iron-on transfers which are great time-savers, are now readily available but, even so, care must be taken to ensure that they are stamped on straight. Before marking, lay out the fabric and secure firmly to keep it flat and taut.

With the dots in place, take a long thread and fasten securely at the beginning of the first horizontal row of dots. Gather along the line going from dot to dot and leaving a length of thread at the far end. Repeat this procedure for all the rows. Pull up the threads and secure every two rows by wrapping the threads around a pin. This will give the material a regular, pleated effect.

Begin at the right hand side and sew the first two pleats together level with the first row of horizontal stitches. Then, working across the fabric, sew the second and third pleats together, half-way between the two rows of stitching. Return to the top row of stitching and sew together the third and fourth pleats. Repeat the process to the end of the row and secure the thread. Go back to the right hand side of the top of the second line of horizontal stitching and start again, sewing as before. If you wish, you can use different coloured threads. This gives a very pretty effect.

Tucking

Tucking controls fullness by gathering the fabric up into a series of flat folds which are stitched into place. Tucks vary in size according to the type of garment. Pin tucks are the smallest and prettiest tucks, being approximately 3mm ($\frac{1}{8}$in) to 6mm ($\frac{1}{4}$in) wide. They are used on fine delicate fabrics and are perfect for the bodice of a small child's dress or on a shirt. Tucks would obviously be wider on skirts and loose-fitting tops and dresses. In general, the amount of material required is three times the width of the tuck to allow for both sides of the tuck and the fabric it covers. However, if the tucks are spaced apart with the space

Fabric gathered ready for smocking

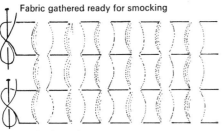

Smocking in progress

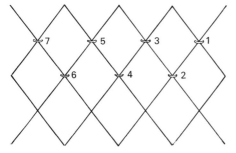

in between the tucks equal to the width of the tuck, only twice the amount of fabric will be required.

The easiest way to prepare the fabric for tucking is to make a gauge out of cardboard or thick paper, cutting notches to mark the width of the tuck (1) and the space between the tucks (2). Transfer these markings on to the fabric. Place the two outer marks of the width of the tuck together and press along the foldline. Pin and tack the tucks across the area to be tucked and then sew firmly into place, either by hand using a small running stitch, or by machine. Pin tucks, on the other hand, should be stitched normally close to the folded edge.

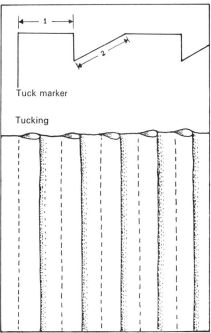

Tuck marker

Tucking

Pleats

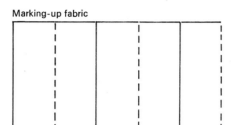

Knife pleats

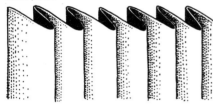

Box pleat

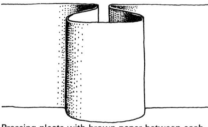

Pressing pleats with brown paper between each pleat

Pleats are yet another way to control fullness and can be used on all kinds of material. They are prepared in a very similar manner to tucking, but a little more time and patience is needed for the accurate marking and tacking required, which is the secret of perfect pleating. In general, the amount of fabric required is three times the finished width.

On the wrong side of the fabric, using tailor's chalk, draw a series of alternate broken and solid vertical lines across the area to be pleated. Take great care to keep the lines straight and an equal distance apart. It will save time if the pleats are made from the wrong side of the fabric, otherwise the pleat markings will have to be transferred to the right side of the fabric with tacking stitches.

With the right sides of the material together, match up the solid line to the broken line of each pleat. Pin the top, bottom and centre of each pleat to hold it straight and then place pins at 2.5cm (2in) intervals along the pleat. Beginning at the lower edge, tack by hand along the chalk mark to the top with even tacking stitches, removing the pins as you tack. Tacking on the wrong side will also prevent the fabric from being marked when the pleats are pressed.

There are several kinds of pleats but probably the most useful for children's clothes are either knife pleats or soft unpressed pleats for pretty skirts ; and either box pleats or pressed pleats for school uniforms. With knife pleats, the pleats are arranged so that the top edge of one pleat meets the under edge of the next one, giving a concertina effect, and the pleats go from right to

edge of the pleat with tailor's chalk and then flatten out the fabric so that the marking is in the centre on top of the tacking. For pressed pleats, work from the wrong side of the fabric and press the inside foldline of each pleat before it is turned to one side. Place the pleat in the right direction and pin the foldline to the skirt at the upper edge. Tack into position with even tacking stitches 1.3cm ($\frac{1}{2}$in) below the cut edge. Turn to the right side of the fabric and press each pleat on the outside edge. It is a good idea to place a strip of brown paper between the pleats when pressing to prevent the crease marking the adjoining pleat.

A pleated skirt in wool, wool-blends, or their synthetic counterparts, makes a warm and pretty addition to a little girl's winter wardrobe. Plain and checked fabrics are equally attractive and, of course, tartan for a kilt. Hem the lower edge before pleating the fabric. Decide on the size of the pleats allowing three times the width for each pleat. Pleat up the fabric to fit the child's waist comfortably and join to a self-fabric waistband. In a kilt, the fabric will have a plain wrap-over in front and a wide piece of fabric should extend underneath to form the underwrap. The waistband should fasten at the edge of the underwrap and at the edge of the wrapover, the side fastening with a kilt pin.

left around the waist. For unpressed pleats work from the wrong side of the fabric. Match up the chalk markings and tack. Pin the fold edge of each pleat to the skirt with pins going vertically and tack into place with even tacking stitches 1.3cm ($\frac{1}{2}$in) below the cut edge. From the wrong side, box pleats resemble two knife pleats facing each other, one turned towards the right and the other towards the left. The quickest and easiest way to make these pleats is to tack a pleat twice the width of the finished pleat. Mark the

Collars

Collars can be very useful for children's clothes, providing a pretty finishing touch to a basic dress, a new look to a shirt or dress handed down from an elder brother or sister and, as children are quickly bored with clothes, a collar adding a different look can give a new lease of life to an outfit which still has plenty of wear left in it. Collars on little boys' shirts and young girls' blouses tend to wear out faster than the main part of the garment. These can be easily replaced, which saves buying a new shirt or blouse. A dainty lace edging around the collar and embroidery on the points looks most attractive. This can turn a girl's simple blouse into a pretty party outfit and makes a perfect pageboy's shirt for a boy. Collars require very little fabric and can be made from left-over pieces of self-fabric from the original garment or remnants of a compatible contrasting material.

Peter Pan Collar

A Peter Pan collar is commonly seen on children's clothes and is one of the easiest to make. It is useful, too, as it can be attached so that the edges meet either at the back or front of the dress or blouse. This collar lies very flat and the neck edge of the collar is the same shape as the neck edge of the garment. The secret of applying this type of collar successfully is to match up these shapes exactly. Carefully fold the garment in half and pin the neck edge to keep the shape in place. Tack and remove the pins. Place a piece of paper on a flat, hard working surface and position the back fold of the outfit level with the edge of the paper. Secure with pins, one at the neck edge and the other 7.5cm (3in) below. Smooth out the garment and pin down the front of the outfit in the same way. With a sharp pencil draw the outline of the neck edge and about 10cm (4in) down the centre front fold. Remove the garment and decide on the desired depth of the collar. This will really depend on the size of the child as too large a collar will swamp a small child and look ridiculous. Conversely, too small a collar on a plump child is unflattering. Mark the width with a series of dots measured from the neck curve. When joined up, they will form a curve parallel to the neckline. In order to prevent a point occurring at the centre back, draw the beginning of the curve at ninety degrees to the edge of the paper. To form the front edge of the collar mark a point 1.3cm ($\frac{1}{2}$in) beyond the centre front on the outer edge of the collar. Join this point with the centre front on the inside edge. Mark the centre back of the collar with tailor's chalk or tacking thread to avoid confusion with the centre front once the pattern piece has been cut out.

Measure from the centre back of the pattern piece to the end of the shape in a straight line to ascertain the amount of fabric required. If you are short of fabric the under collar can be made from a compatible contrasting fabric or from lining material. Fold the fabric on the crosswise grain and pin the centre back edge to the fold. Cut out once or twice according to whether the under collar is to be cut from the same fabric or not, allowing sufficient for a seam allowance around the edges. Mark the

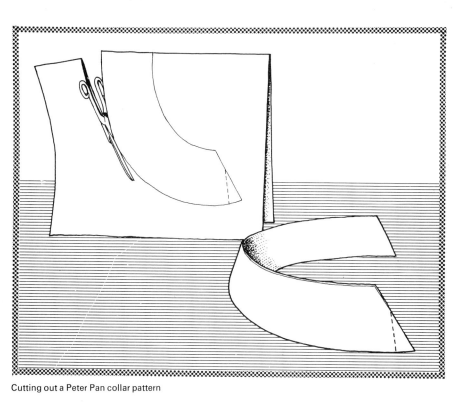

Cutting out a Peter Pan collar pattern

centre front and the centre back of the collar. Cut a piece of interfacing the same size as the collar and pin to the wrong side of the under collar. Tack into place on the seamline and cut diagonally across the corners of the interfacing only 6mm ($\frac{1}{4}$in) inside the seam allowance. With right sides together sew the under and upper collars together leaving the neck edge open. Cut the interfacing close to the stitching-line and grade the seams leaving the widest amount of fabric on the upper collar. Cut the corners diagonally and clip the curves. Turn the collar through to the right side and press. Tack the neck edges together on the seamline.

On the right side of the garment, tack the collar into place with the under collar next to the outfit and matching centre front and centre back. Pin the facing or a bias strip of fabric over the collar, tack and remove the pins. Sew through all thicknesses on the seam. Remove the tacking stitches, grade the seam allowances and clip curves. Press the facing to the inside of the garment and slip stitch into place. If you would prefer the collar opening to the centre back instead of the centre front, the process is reversed and the centre front edge is placed to the edge of the paper when making the pattern piece and then to the fold edge of the fabric.

Collars

Two other sorts of collar often seen in children's clothes are the more tailored roll collar and the decorative mandarin collar.

Roll Collar

A roll collar gives a neat tailored look to a dress, blouse or shirt, but is much easier to apply than a proper shirt collar which is attached to a neckband first. The secret of making a collar roll or turn back correctly without the edges curling up is to cut the upper collar slightly bigger than the undercollar. The neck edge is the same but about 3mm ($\frac{1}{8}$in) should be added all around the outer edges of light and medium weight fabrics and about 6mm ($\frac{1}{4}$in) to thicker fabrics. The interfacing is sewn to the wrong side of the under collar and the two collar pieces are then joined together as described for a Peter Pan collar. However, when the collar is turned through to the right side, roll the edge of the upper collar to the underside when pressing so that the seamline does not show. With the top collar facing upwards, shape the collar before attaching it to the neckline by rolling the upper collar over the edge of your hand and pinning along the line on which the collar turns back just above the seamline. Tack the neck edges together and you will find the top collar will lie back just short of the edge of the under collar. Pin to the right side of the garment with the under collar next to the outfit. Tack the facing over the top and sew through all thicknesses. Grade the seam allowances and clip the curves.

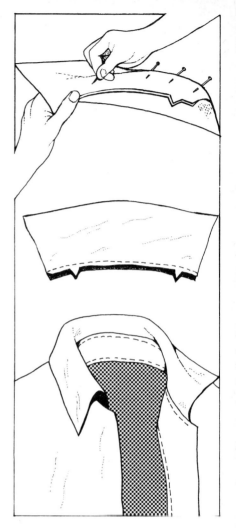

Press the seam towards the facing and understitch, finishing about 5cm (2in) from the edges, to prevent the facing being pulled out. Turn the facing to the inside of the garment, press and catch stitch to the garment seams, being careful not to catch in the outer fabric so that the stitches show through to the right side.

Mandarin Collar

A mandarin collar is cut on the straight grain of the fabric in one rectangular piece twice the finished width of the collar and attached to the curved neckline with a shaped facing. Mark the centre or foldline of the collar and cut a piece of interfacing half the size of the collar fabric. Join the interfacing to the wrong side of half the collar section, tacking it on the seamline and slip stitching it to the centre foldline. Cut the corners of the interfacing 6mm ($\frac{1}{4}$in) inside the seam allowance. Fold the collar in half lengthwise and machine the short side seams. Cut the interfacing close to the stitching-line, grade the seam allowances and cut the corners diagonally. Turn the collar through to the right side and press. Tack the neck edges together on the seamline. However, if curved corners are desired rather than square ones, the collar has to be constructed in two parts and the under and upper collars joined as previously described. Pin the collar to the neck edge of the garment and tack into place on the seamline. Pin and tack the facing over the top of the collar, right sides together and sew through all thicknesses. Cut the interfacing close to the stitching-line, grade the seam allowances and clip curves. It will be necessary to understitch the facing and collar seams together to prevent the facing rolling back towards the collar. Press the facing to the inside and slip stitch it to the shoulder seams.

Mandarin collar

(*Opposite*) To make a roll collar : roll the upper collar back from seamline and pin along seamline ; tack raw edges together ; attach collar to garment

Simple Pockets

Pockets are most essential for children's clothes. Of course, they are useful for the necessities of life such as hankies, pocket money or bus fares, and sweets, but children are like squirrels when it comes to collecting things during the day and what better place to hide them than in a pocket. You can make pockets out of left-over fabric from the garment or you can have patch pockets which look very attractive made in contrasting materials. Embroidery motifs and appliqué give a very pretty finishing touch to pockets.

Pockets are quite easy to make. Decide on the size required and allow 2.5cm (1in) at the top and about a 1cm ($\frac{3}{8}$in) seam around the other edges. Neaten the raw edges either by hand or with a machine zig-zag stitch and turn down the top edge on the 2.5cm (1in) hem allowed to the outside of the pocket. Starting at the folded edge stitch on the 1cm ($\frac{3}{8}$in) seamline around the pocket. Cut the corners at the top diagonally and clip the curves if making a rounded pocket. Turn the top hem to the inside and turn in on the stitching-line. Mitre the corners on a square pocket. Tack the seams and press. Pin the pocket to the garment. Tack and remove the pins. Sew into position close to the edge of the pocket, remove the tacking stitches and press. Curved pockets are probably best for children as they tend to collect dust less quickly than the corners of square ones.

If a pocket is going to be in constant use rather than just being decorative, it is a good idea to line it as this will help to preserve its shape. Cut the lining the same size as the pocket up to the bottom of the hem flap plus a 1.3cm ($\frac{1}{2}$in) seam allowance. With right sides together, pin the upper edges of the lining and the pocket together. Stitch along the seam allowance leaving a 2.5cm (1in) opening in the centre so that the pocket can be turned through to the right side. Press the seam towards the lining. With right sides together, fold the pocket on the hemline marking and pin. Stitch the lining and the hem allowance to the pocket around the outer edges. Grade the seam allowances and cut the corners diagonally. Turn the pocket to the right side, carefully pulling out the corners with a pin. Slip stitch the opening and press the pocket. Pin the pocket to the garment. Tack into place and remove the pins. Sew the pockets close to the edge by machine or slip stitch by hand. Remove the tacking stitches and press.

A little boy may prefer to have a pocket in the side seam of his trousers. This is quite easy to do during construction; the pocket should be inserted before the side seam is sewn up. First decide on the depth of the pocket opening and the width required. For a small child about 12.5cm (5in) deep would be sufficient. With a paper and pencil draw a vertical line 12.5cm (5in) long and another line 9cm ($3\frac{1}{2}$in) long at right angles to this. Mark a spot 2.5cm (1in) below the bottom of the vertical line. Draw a curved line joining the top and bottom point slightly slanting so that the bottom of the pocket extends below the bottom of the opening. Cut out two pocket

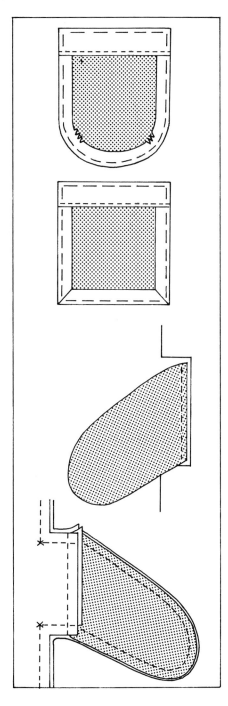

shapes either from self-fabric, if you have any to spare, or from lining material. Extend the seam allowances on the trousers by 2cm ($\frac{3}{4}$in) continuing 1.5cm ($\frac{5}{8}$in) above and below where the pocket is to be inserted. On the original seamline, mark 1.5cm ($\frac{5}{8}$in) in from the top and bottom edges of the extension either with tailor's chalk or tacking stitches. On the wrong side of the fabric sew one pocket to one seam extension and the other pocket to the other extension. Press both seams towards the pocket. The side seams of the trousers and the pockets are sewn together at the same time. Begin from the top of the trouser leg and, when you reach the 1.5cm ($\frac{5}{8}$in) mark at the top of the pocket opening in the seamline, release the tension, if sewing by machine, and swivel the fabric around so that you are ready to start sewing up the pocket. Replace the foot and sew around the outside of the two pocket shapes. When you reach the bottom 1.5cm ($\frac{5}{8}$in) mark, once again release the tension and swivel the fabric around. Replace the foot and continue to sew the rest of the side seam.

(*From the top*) Round pocket seen from the wrong side ; patch pocket seen from the wrong side with edges turned in, ready to apply to garment ; inserting a pocket into a side seam

Simple Skirts

A simple gathered skirt is a pretty and practical addition to a little girl's wardrobe, as it can be worn with many different T-shirts, blouses and sweaters, thus providing several outfits from one basic garment. It is easy to make, too, as the only part where fitting is required is around the waist. Choose a plain fabric or one with an overall design so that there is no need to worry about matching the seam. Also choose a soft material which will gather easily, such as a lightweight cotton, cotton blend, lightweight wool, a wool blend, and the synthetic counterparts.

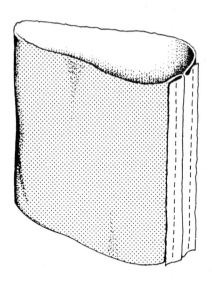

The amount of material required is approximately one and a half times the waist measurement or twice the amount if a really full skirt is desired. Test on a sample piece of fabric first to see how much fullness is required as a thin child will benefit from the extra width afforded by a very full skirt and a chubbier child will be better off with less gathers.

There are three quick and easy ways of making the skirt. It can be either made all in one with an elastic casing at the top; gathered into a self-fabric waistband; or, if you are short of fabric, gathered on to decorative elastic. In all cases allow as large a hem as the fullness will allow without looking bulky, so that this can be let down as the child grows. Again this can be tested first on a sample piece of material.

When an elastic casing is used to control the fullness, measure the finished length required plus the hem allowance and 2.2cm ($\frac{7}{8}$in) at the top for the casing. Turn under 6mm ($\frac{1}{4}$in) to the wrong side of the fabric at the top edge and press. With right sides together, join the side seam taking a 1.5cm ($\frac{5}{8}$in) seam allowance. Press the seam open and neaten the raw edges. Turn under 1.5cm ($\frac{5}{8}$in) at the top edge and stitch very close to the foldline. Stitch again close to the bottom edge leaving a 2.5cm (1in) gap through which to insert the elastic. Cut a length of 1.3cm ($\frac{1}{2}$in) wide elastic so that it fits comfortably around the waist plus an extra 1.5cm ($\frac{1}{2}$in). Attach a safety pin to one end of the elastic and thread it through the casing. Overlap the ends of the elastic by 6mm ($\frac{1}{4}$in) on each end and sew together securely. Hem the remainder of the opening in the casing. Turn up the hem.

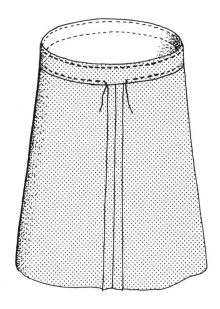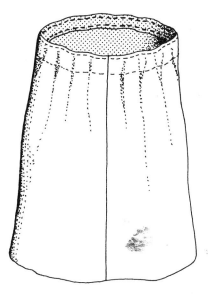

When joining a gathered skirt to a waistband of decorative elastic or one of self-fabric, again measure the finished length of the skirt plus the hem and a 1.5cm ($\frac{5}{8}$in) seam allowance at the top edge. Gather up the fabric to the required width with two rows of gathering stitches, one on the 1.5cm ($\frac{5}{8}$in) seamline and the other 6mm ($\frac{1}{4}$in) above this in the seam allowance, leaving 1.5cm ($\frac{5}{8}$in) seam allowance at each side of the gathers. Adjust the gathers evenly. With right sides together join the two sides taking a 1.5cm ($\frac{5}{8}$in) seam and finishing 11.5cm ($4\frac{5}{8}$in) below the top edge. Tack up the remainder of the seam and press open the seam. Insert a 10cm (4in) zip with the zip head ending 1.5cm ($\frac{5}{8}$in) below the top of the skirt. Remove the tacking threads. Join the skirt to the waistband.

Making a simple gathered skirt
(*From left to right*) join side seam ; leave a gap in lower stitching of waistband to insert elastic ; finished skirt

Skirts and Waistbands

If you wish to use decorative elastic for the waistband, first cut a length of the elastic so that it fits comfortably around the waist, plus an extra 2cm ($\frac{3}{4}$in). Turn in 3mm ($\frac{1}{8}$in) at either end of the elastic to neaten the raw edges. Lap the elastic over the gathered skirt fabric just covering the bottom row of gathers. Pin and tack into position with the left side parallel to the left side of the zip opening and the right-hand end extending by 1.3cm ($\frac{1}{2}$in). Machine on the seamline through the bottom row of gathers, catching in the elastic. Sew snaps or hooks and eyes under the overlap on the elastic to hold the waistband in place. Turn up the hem.

To make a self-fabric waistband, cut a length of material so that it fits comfortably around the waist plus 4.5cm ($1\frac{3}{4}$in) by twice the width of the finished waistband plus 3.2cm ($1\frac{1}{4}$in). Cut out the interfacing, making it the same length as the fabric but half as wide. Pin the interfacing to the wrong side of half the waistband. Tack along the long and short sides 1.5cm ($\frac{5}{8}$in) in from the edge and stitch to the centre of the waistband with loose hemming stitches. Cut across the corners of the interfacing diagonally 6mm ($\frac{1}{4}$in) inside the stitching-line. Turn up 1.5cm ($\frac{5}{8}$in) to the wrong side of the other long edge and press. With right sides together, pin the interfaced side of the waistband to the skirt extending the left-hand side by 1.5cm ($\frac{5}{8}$in) and the right-hand side by 2.8cm ($1\frac{1}{8}$in). Stitch into place taking

a 1.5cm ($\frac{5}{8}$in) seam allowance machining through the bottom row of gathers. Trim the interfacing close to the stitching line and grade the seam allowances. Press the seam towards the waistband. Fold the waistband in half with the right sides together and sew the short sides together taking a 1.5cm ($\frac{5}{8}$in) seam. Clip the corners diagonally and grade the seam allowance. Turn the waistband through to the right side and pull out the corners gently with a pin. Hem into place along the 1.5cm ($\frac{5}{8}$in) seamline and press. Sew hooks and eyes or snaps under the overlap to close the waistband. Turn up the hem.

For a smart tailored look, choose an A-line skirt. This is also a more flattering line for a plump child than a gathered skirt whose fullness is more beneficial to a thin child. It is easy to make if you choose one with two side seams. Shaping is usually given by waist darts and the skirt fastens with a zip in the side seam. The skirt can be attached to a fabric waistband in the same way as a gathered skirt, or the waistline edge can be finished easily by using a grosgrain ribbon facing. Use 1.5cm ($\frac{5}{8}$in) wide ribbon and cut a piece long enough to fit your child's waist comfortably plus a 1.5cm ($\frac{5}{8}$in) extension beyond the front edge and 1.3cm ($\frac{1}{2}$in) beyond the back edge of the zip. With right sides up, pin the grosgrain ribbon to the waist seamline, extending beyond the edges as described and edge stitch to the waistline. Cut the skirt fabric to 6mm ($\frac{1}{4}$in) from the stitching-line. Turn in the edges of the ribbon and hem stitch to the tapes of the zip. Turn up the hem.

Further reading from David & Charles

GOOD FOOD GROWING GUIDE
Gardening and Living Nature's Way
John Bond and the Staff of 'Mother Earth'
A new-look growing guide to healthier and happier living
241 × 148mm   illustrated

ECONOMY COOK BOOK
Mary Griffiths
A guide to how to cope with rising food and housekeeping prices and still produce tasty and nutritious meals
216 × 138mm

COST-EFFECTIVE SELF-SUFFICIENCY
or The Middle-Class Peasant
Eve and Terence McLaughlin
A practical guide to self-sufficiency, proving that life as 'middle-class peasants' is not only viable but enormously enjoyable and satisfying
247 × 171mm   illustrated

EAT CHEAPLY AND WELL
Brenda Sanctuary
Rising food prices make this up-to-the-minute book a must for today's housewives
216 × 138mm   illustrated

GROWPLAN VEGETABLE BOOK
A Month-by-Month Guide
Peter Peskett and Geoff Amos
A practical, easy-reference guide to growing super vegetables, and fruit too, month by month
250 × 200mm   illustrated

GROWING FOOD UNDER GLASS:
1001 Questions Answered
Adrienne and Peter Oldale
An indispensable guide to setting up and maintaining every kind of glasshouse, together with an A–Z rundown of the familiar and unusual fruit and vegetables to be grown
210 × 148mm   illustrated

GROWING FRUIT:
1001 Questions Answered
Adrienne and Peter Oldale
Answers all the questions a novice might ask about pests and diseases, choice of tree shapes and varieties, and pruning techniques
210 × 148mm   illustrated

GROWING VEGETABLES:
1001 Questioned Answered
Adrienne and Peter Oldale
All you need to know about growing vegetables in a simple question and answer format
210 × 148mm   illustrated

COMPLETE BOOK OF HERBS AND SPICES
Claire Loewenfeld and Philippa Back
A comprehensive guide to every aspect of herbs and spices—their history and traditions, cultivation, uses in the kitchen, and health and cosmetics
242 × 184mm   illustrated

COOK OUT
Frances Kitchin
For the cook on a caravanning or camping holiday, Frances Kitchin provides the answers to all the problems when cooking meals with the minimum of facilities
210 × 132mm   illustrated

British Library Cataloguing in Publication Data
Fox, Gail
Making your children's clothes.—(Penny pinchers).
1. Children's clothing
I. Title II. Series
646.4'06   TT635

ISBN 0–7153–7549–0

First published 1978
Second impression 1979

Set in Univers
and printed in Great Britain
by Redwood Burn Limited
for David & Charles (Publishers) Limited
Brunel House   Newton Abbot   Devon

Published in the United States of America
by David & Charles Inc
North Pomfret   Vermont 05053   USA